COLONIAL NEW ENGLAND
ON 5 SHILLINGS A DAY

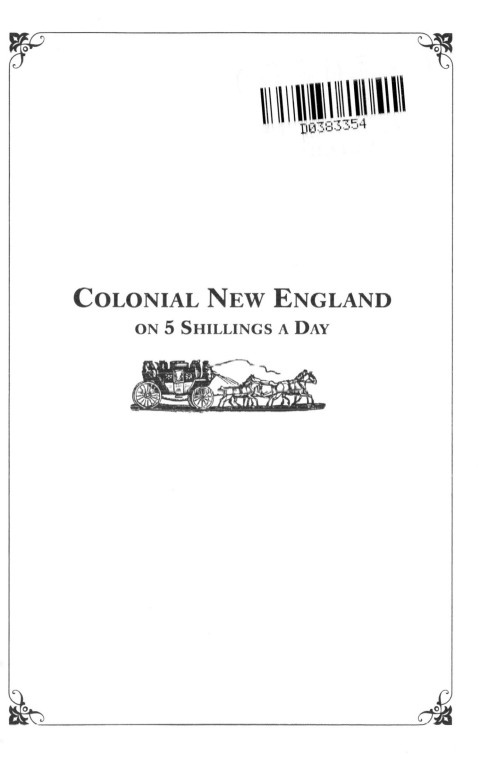

BILL SCHELLER

COLONIAL NEW ENGLAND
ON 5 SHILLINGS A DAY

WITH 89 ILLUSTRATIONS, 8 IN COLOR

Thames & Hudson

CONTENTS

PREFACE

"New England," the historian Bernard DeVoto wrote in 1932, "is a finished place ... It is the first American section to be finished, to achieve stability in the conditions of its life." In the nearly eighty years since DeVoto made that observation, there have been more than a few changes in the conditions of New England's life. But in many ways it does give the appearance of having been "finished" some time ago – perhaps as far back as the mid-eighteenth century, the time in which travelers might have found this guide a useful companion. The political geography has changed hardly at all: here are Massachusetts, Connecticut, Rhode Island, and New Hampshire with very nearly their exact modern borders; as for Vermont and Maine, which were not colonies in their own right, their boundaries were less precise only because their northernmost reaches were wilderness surveyed poorly if at all.

New England offers many visual touchstones. With its white steeples, village greens encircled by trim clapboard houses, and narrow streets that carry the tang of salt air inland from ancient harbors, it's easy to see why today's visitors have little trouble conjuring the eighteenth century.

Although we'll occasionally refer to later events, our time in this guide is the early to middle 1760s. Discontent with certain aspects of British rule is growing, although hardly anyone in New England desires or foresees independence. For most, the hardscrabble life of the "Pilgrim century" – the 1600s – is only a memory; and the well-to-do enjoy a sophisticated style of living that many Europeans might have envied. The region's population stands at around 425,000, enough to make these colonies one of the bulwarks of what will later be known as the "old" British Empire, held together by oaken hulls and sailcloth. Still well in the future are the days of New England's own maritime prowess, and its rise as a textile empire built on the profits of the China Trade.

But for now, circa 1760–66, New England is indeed a finished place.

I

GETTING THERE
– AND SOME PRACTICAL TIPS

New Englanders are well set in their good opinion of themselves and their little corner of America – so much so that if you were to ask them how to get to New England, they might tell you that the best policy is to be there already. But since not everyone can be so fortunate, it's good to know what's involved in making the trip – whether from England, or from the more southerly American colonies.

There's no getting around the fact that passage across the Atlantic is not for the fainthearted. Although a well-manned merchant vessel with an experienced crew (not to mention fair winds) can make the crossing from London, Liverpool, or Cowes in as little as four weeks, there's always the chance that you'll be at sea twice as long, and even longer if you've sailed from Rotterdam or one of the other continental ports.

Ships prepare to sail from London's Old East India Wharf, 1750s.

It will be a good half-century before the packet schooners begin sailing on a more or less regular schedule between Boston and Great Britain. But there's never a shortage of merchant vessels making the voyage, as commerce between the New World and the Old has increased steadily throughout the eighteenth century. Captains are more than happy to take on as many passengers as they can manage, and it's a rare ship that doesn't carry at least a few colonial officials, merchants, hopeful emigrants, and travelers with time and curiosity to spare.

But unless you're a shipowner, high official, or a person of means, you'll do well to remember that you and your fellow passengers are not nearly as important as the cargo in the hold. You will, in fact, *feel* like cargo in the hold, when you see what sort of accommodations your £5 or so have purchased. Listen to what a divinity student named Jacob Bailey had to say about the quarters he was assigned, on a merchantman making the voyage between Boston and London in 1760: "I followed [another passenger] down a ladder into a dark and dismal region, where the fumes of pitch, bilge water, and other kinds of nastiness almost suffocated me in a minute ... We entered a small apartment, hung round with damp and greasy canvas, which made, on every hand, a most gloomy and frightful appearance. In the middle stood a table of pine, varnished over with nasty slime, furnished with a bottle of rum and an old tin mug with a hundred and fifty bruises and holes, through which the liquid poured in as many streams ... This detestable apartment was allotted by the Captain to be the place of my habitation during the voyage."

At least young Bailey had rum to wash down the food – and from all accounts of shipboard cuisine, the more rum the better. Salt beef, potatoes, and onions will probably make up the bulk of your provisions, which might not even be included in the price of your passage. It's no wonder that wealthier passengers bring their own food for the transatlantic voyage.

"All this misery reaches its climax when in addition to everything else one must also suffer through two to three days and nights of storm, with everyone convinced that the ship with all aboard is bound to sink. In such misery all the people on board pray and cry pitifully together."

FROM AN ANONYMOUS PASSENGER'S ACCOUNT,
MID-EIGHTEENTH CENTURY

If you're traveling from the middle Atlantic or southern American colonies, you'll at least have the advantage of a shorter trip, even if the table is set no more elegantly. From Charleston or Savannah, expect a sail of a week to ten days before you reach Boston; from Philadelphia, count on five. With favorable winds, a good coastal trading vessel can cover the distance from New York to the Massachusetts capital in three days. The voyage from

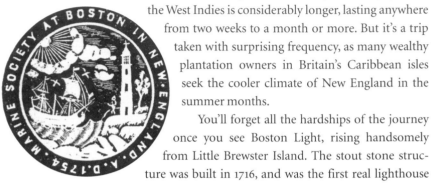

the West Indies is considerably longer, lasting anywhere from two weeks to a month or more. But it's a trip taken with surprising frequency, as many wealthy plantation owners in Britain's Caribbean isles seek the cooler climate of New England in the summer months.

You'll forget all the hardships of the journey once you see Boston Light, rising handsomely from Little Brewster Island. The stout stone structure was built in 1716, and was the first real lighthouse in New England. It replaced the pot of pitch that was set ablaze each night on the loftiest part of Boston's Trimount

Boston Light, a welcome sight for mariners.

– the summit that thus got the name of Beacon Hill. Beneath the copper roof of Boston Light, safe behind glass, are lamps supplied with oil several times each night, and trimmed every hour by the lonely and dedicated keeper.

Of course, you can also travel by land. A *mostly* reliable system of post roads now stretches from Savannah in the colony of Georgia to Portsmouth, the handsome capital of New Hampshire. Few travelers will want to cover all of that distance by coach, ferrying across a dozen rivers or more, and trusting to inns that turn up only infrequently south of Philadelphia. But the overland route from New York into New England is a popular one, especially if the destination is New Haven or Hartford in Connecticut, or Springfield in the western part of Massachusetts. We'll take a longer look at what the overland traveler can expect in Chapter Five.

A coach and four, suitable for colonial New England's better roads.

What Currency to Use?

This seems like it should be a simple question – since the New England colonies are British possessions, shouldn't the pound sterling should be the universal currency? Yes and no. Sterling is accepted throughout the four colonies and their dependencies, and locally minted coinage (each colony has its own) is based on the British system. But the Spanish dollar is usually just as acceptable as the coin of the realm. In many places, it's the main currency used in daily commerce; in others, the Dutch guilder or French sou might turn up in American pockets and cash drawers.

But money matters in New England get even more complicated. In Britain, a Spanish milled dollar – also known as a "piece of eight" – is generally worth between 4s. 3d. and 4s. 9d. In the colonies, that same dollar can be worth as much as 8s., and even British coins can trade at a higher rate of exchange. Keep this in mind as you budget for your trip, but remember: many items are more expensive in the colonies because of import costs. If you buy locally made goods, you'll be more likely to benefit from the inflated value of Spanish or British currency.

And whatever coins are in your pocket, just be glad that you aren't the tavern keeper making change out of all these conflicting denominations.

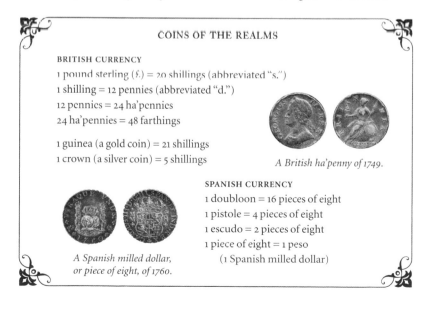

COINS OF THE REALMS

BRITISH CURRENCY
1 pound sterling (£.) = 20 shillings (abbreviated "s.")
1 shilling = 12 pennies (abbreviated "d.")
12 pennies = 24 ha'pennies
24 ha'pennies = 48 farthings

1 guinea (a gold coin) = 21 shillings
1 crown (a silver coin) = 5 shillings

A British ha'penny of 1749.

SPANISH CURRENCY
1 doubloon = 16 pieces of eight
1 pistole = 4 pieces of eight
1 escudo = 2 pieces of eight
1 piece of eight = 1 peso
(1 Spanish milled dollar)

A Spanish milled dollar,
or piece of eight, of 1760.

What Will it Cost?

It's possible to live quite comfortably while traveling in New England for 5s. a day, give or take a few pence. As an example of what decent lodgings and meals are likely to cost, let's look at typical charges at one of the most pleasant inns in the Massachusetts countryside, the Red Horse Tavern on the Post Road in Sudbury, about 25 miles west of Boston. Mr. Ezekiel Howe, the proprietor, offers the following schedule of charges (a mug of Mr. Howe's excellent India flip will add 15d. to the tariff, for a total of 5s. 9d.):

One night's lodging:	4d.
Breakfast	15d.
Dinner	20d.
Supper	15d.
Total	4s. 6d.

MR. HOWE'S FLIP

Two ounces West Indies rum
One teaspoon sugar
Four ounces milk
One egg

Briskly mix the egg with the rum and sugar, and pour into a mug. Top with milk, and stir. If you are lucky enough to have a nutmeg (not the wooden kind, which unscrupulous Connecticut peddlers are said to sell), grate it atop your flip.

Our figures do not take into account the cost of moving about by coach, or of the care and feeding of your horse if that is your means of travel. And New England is no different than the Old World when it comes to city living: put up at a good inn in Boston, or Newport, or Portsmouth, and your bed and meals – not to mention your India flip – will likely cost more than in the countryside.

INFLATION MARCHES ON

Economic historians estimate that £750 in mid-eighteenth-century Massachusetts was the equivalent of around $62,000 in 2009 dollars.

What to Expect from the Weather

That's an easy question to answer – New Englanders don't expect anything from the weather, since it changes so frequently. But the one thing you can count on are extremes. New England can be hot and humid in summer, and bitterly cold in winter. Temperatures moderate a bit along the seacoasts in both seasons, although the dampness and ocean breeze can chill you to the bone from November through April. An especially good time to stay close to the tavern hearth is when the shoreline gets hit with what New Englanders call a "Nor'easter," a ferocious storm that bears down from, that's right, the northeast, with rain, sleet, snow, and whatever other shape cold water might take, along with high tides that are all the worse when the moon is full. The men who fish for cod out of ports like Gloucester and New Bedford, or who set out from Nantucket on whaling ships, fear the Nor'easter more than any kind of weather, and you'll be lucky to be safe in port before the season starts.

If you head inland during the winter, you should be prepared for snow such as you've never seen in Britain or Europe, or in the southern American colonies. In the hinterlands of Massachusetts and New Hampshire, and especially in the wilds of Maine and that remote, contested place called Vermont (it's claimed by both New Hampshire and New York), snow can bury a dwelling to its eaves, and make what few roads there are impossible to travel. In those dark forests and rugged mountains, spring stays a stranger until well into May, and the snows begin again in late October. The growing season is so short in these northern wastes, that it is unlikely farming can ever flourish there, even now that the French and their Indian allies no longer bedevil the region's hardy settlers.

Spring is a short season in New England, and the weather is pleasant – though May and June, in country places, can be plagued by clouds of black flies that drive man and beast to distraction. But if there is a truly special time in these colonies, it is autumn, when the trees put on such a display of color that unaccustomed travelers sometimes ask if the local forests are diseased. They are perfectly healthy; yet somehow, a quirk of the New England climate, or of the soil, turns the maples red, the birches yellow, and the oaks a ruddy bronze. Enjoy the color while you can – already, in the settled districts of New England, so many trees have been cut to clear the land for farming that firewood must be sent by ship to Boston from the virgin forests of Maine.

WHAT SHOULD YOU BRING TO WEAR?

Travelers should keep the changes of the seasons in mind when packing for a trip to New England. Because the Atlantic passage takes so long, and few will want to turn right around to make the homeward voyage, it's likely that a sojourn here will last over the course of two seasons or more. So, there's not much sense in thinking about packing light.

If you're bringing along a foul-weather suit of oiled canvas for going above-decks on shipboard, it will serve you well in a New England storm, except in the depth of winter (and if you haven't such an item, you can pick one up from a colonial clothier for 7 or 8s.). For really fierce winter weather, men and women alike ought to have a thick woolen cloak or greatcoat. Remember, there was a good reason that a New England traveler once asked if he were riding in a coach, or a hollowed-out iceberg.

Changes in weather are one reason for carrying an ample and varied wardrobe. And if you're planning to spend time both in the New England countryside and in the cities, you've got quite another reason. Aside from what you may have heard at home about American colonials being a bunch of rustics who don't know how to turn themselves out in style, city life in New England has become quite sophisticated, even by London standards (and by the standards of those southern planters who set themselves up as British landed gentry). If you have any doubts, just take a look at the portrait of Nicholas Boylston, the Boston merchant prince, lately painted by up-and-coming young artist John Singleton Copley (see Plate I). Boylston's exquisite dressing gown of green brocaded silk makes one wonder what he might wear for a social evening, if this is what he throws on at home when he isn't even wearing his wig.

BEWIGGED, OR NOT TO BE?

Forgot your wig? Don't worry – there are plenty of wigmakers in the larger New England towns, especially in Boston. In all but the most formal circles, though, you won't be faulted for adopting the increasingly popular fashion of going wigless, and powdering your own hair. When you do wear a wig, short and simple is becoming the rule. Expect to pay £1 12s. or thereabouts, perhaps more if you've specified human rather than horse or goat hair.

Copley's portrait of dapper John Hancock.

Men won't be expected to dress like Boylston, or like Thomas Hancock and his elegant young nephew John, to cut a decent figure in a Boston drawing room. But a few city basics are in order. Plan on packing at least one good dress coat, close-fitting in the upper body and in the current collarless style. Your British velvet or silk taffeta coat will mark you as a gentleman of taste and style, but few would look down on a fine wool broadcloth – the fabric New Englanders themselves often choose when visiting their tailors for a fitting.

For less formal wear, and general outdoor use in all but the worst weather, bring along a less form fitting frock coat of linen or wool, depending on the season. Deep pockets, and a collar to turn up against the weather, make the frock coat ideal for travel, for country rambles, and for daytime wanderings in town. And with either a dress or a frock coat, you'll want a smart, close fitting waistcoat. Bring two – single-breasted for evenings in town, and double-breasted to wear with your frock while spending time outdoors. It's a good idea to carry several pairs of breeches, too, ranging from a serviceable coarse wool or canvas, to dress breeches of finer wool or linen.

Bring along enough linen shirts to see you through from one laundress to another. Soiled linen can always be concealed, at the neck, with a simple pleated stock, just now replacing the fussier linen cravats among fashion trendsetters, and more practical for travel. And, also for practicality's sake, save your long, ruffled shirt cuffs for city evening wear.

ALMOST UP TO DATE

In general, fashions in New England are never more than a year behind those in Britain.

Even more so than men, women travelers to New England will have to think about where they're likely to be spending time – more to the point, where they're likely to be invited – before they decide how many trunks to bring. At the very least, ladies will want to pack a sufficient number of petticoats, along with at least one *robe à la Française* or "sack" gown, regardless of what the smart set may be saying about this style going out of fashion (see Plate II). A good sack gown should be made of fine silk, with ample back pleats flowing from the shoulder, flounced sleeves, and elegant trimmings. Why pack more than one? It depends on where you intend to be seen. It wouldn't do, if you're meeting the cream of New Hampshire society at a ball at Governor Wentworth's Portsmouth mansion, to be caught in the same gown the following week at Captain Samuel Moffatt's fine waterfront residence in the same city.

"I must take notice that this place abounds with pretty women, who appear rather more abroad than they do at [New] York, and dress elegantly."
ALEXANDER HAMILTON (NOT THE STATESMAN), 1744

For everyday wear, several of the simpler *robes à l'Anglaise*, in linen or a lighter silk, will serve you well. But remember New England's climate – in chilly weather, you'll be glad to have packed a sleeveless quilted bodice that fits beneath your gown; the better ones have an inner layer of fleece. Also advisable for cool days is a fitted jacket, skirted at the hip.

For country wear, gentlewomen in New England often favor a riding habit, cut and trimmed like a man's frock coat, but skirted like a gown. Wear one of these with a matching petticoat, and you'll be the perfect model of stylishness and comfort.

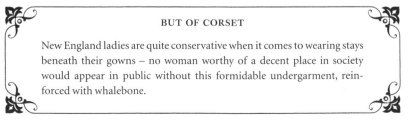

BUT OF CORSET

New England ladies are quite conservative when it comes to wearing stays beneath their gowns – no woman worthy of a decent place in society would appear in public without this formidable undergarment, reinforced with whalebone.

II

A BIT OF HISTORY

New England has been the northern cornerstone of Great Britain's American empire for nearly a century and a half. Beginning with the arrival of the first straggling handful of religious dissenters, the English settlements have grown to become four prosperous and populous colonies. It's only been within the past decade, about 1755, that Philadelphia has overtaken Boston as the largest city in North America.

Although there were several earlier attempts to start a colony in Maine, it was the Pilgrims, at Plymouth in 1620, who planted the first permanent British settlement north of Virginia. They were followed by the founders of Gloucester on Cape Ann in 1623, and Salem in 1628. In 1630, emigrants sponsored by the Massachusetts Bay Company sailed south from Salem and nosed into the

Colonists meet Indians in this detail from a 1755 New England map.

mouth of the Charles River. They found a freshwater spring under the brow of a hill on the Shawmut Peninsula, a scraggly knob of land just barely connected to the mainland by a narrow isthmus. It was here that they founded the town of Boston.

When you visit Boston today, you'll find the outline of that peninsula considerably altered. As the port grew and prospered over the past century, landfill projects smoothed out some of its edges, and made more room for the city's growth. A few visionaries are already talking about shoveling away the summit of Beacon Hill, and dumping it along the shoreline to make even more land. The real dreamers even look to a time when the tidal flats along the Charles River, called the "Back Bay," might be filled and made fit for building. But few Bostonians believe that anyone but wading birds will ever inhabit that dismal, muddy stretch that lies west of the Common.

CROWDED OUT

When the Puritan emigrants arrived on the Shawmut Peninsula in 1630, they found one Englishman already living there – the Reverend William Blaxton. Rev. Blaxton didn't care for so much company, so he packed his books and left for Rhode Island.

"We must Consider that we shall be as a City upon a Hill, the eyes of all people are upon us."

PURITAN LEADER JOHN WINTHROP, ON ARRIVAL
AT BOSTON ABOARD THE *ARBELLA*

Most of the ancestors of today's New Englanders came from the cities and towns of East Anglia, in the southeast part of England, from Dorset in the south, and from the eastern county of Lincolnshire. For their time, they were a highly literate group. It's believed that twice as many of them could read and write as their English countrymen back home.

The great majority of this first generation of settlers, and of the "Great Migration" that followed, were in strong disagreement with the practices and beliefs of the Church of England, which they felt had not rid itself of Roman Catholic influence. Harassed and often persecuted at home – the

Pilgrim settlers of Plymouth had exiled themselves to Holland for ten years before crossing the Atlantic ocean – they sought to found a "new Zion" in the American wilderness.

A PURITAN PRIMER

Calvin inspired English Puritans.

What do Puritans believe? Puritans (the term is not so common now) are Calvinists, accepting the Reformation leader John Calvin's doctrine of humankind's inherent sinfulness, and the predestination of all souls for either salvation, or eternal damnation. They reject pomp and ceremony in religious observations, preferring the long, dire sermons of preachers such as the recently departed Reverend Jonathan Edwards of Northampton, Massachusetts; and they forbade such frivolous celebrations as Christmas. Even today, the twenty-fifth of December is a day like any other for the great majority of New Englanders (see Chapter Nine).

Puritans reject the idea of a church hierarchy, believing that each congregation of believers – and each individual within the congregation – stands in direct communion with God. The term "Congregational" has yet to come into use as the name for this denomination, and, in our mid-century era, the Puritans' descendants simply call their religious institutions "the churches of Christ in New England." The church buildings themselves are usually referred to as "meetinghouses."

THE ORIGINAL NEW ENGLANDERS

The settlers' new Zion was not an uninhabited place. The Pilgrims themselves were greeted by the natives of southern Massachusetts, members of the Wampanoag tribe. Although they were fearful of the Indians, so much so that during their first winter at Plymouth they buried their dead by night to keep the natives from seeing how greatly their numbers had diminished, many more or perhaps all of them would have perished if they had not ultimately been befriended by the Wampanoag sachem (chief) Massasoit and the Patuxent

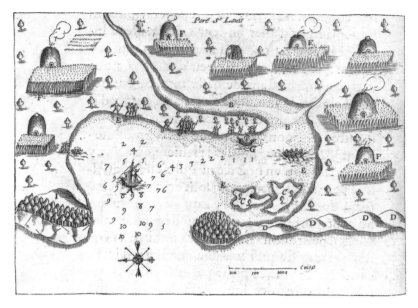

French explorer Samuel de Champlain's depiction of a Wampanoag village near Plymouth, 1605.

Indian Squanto. Squanto, who had been captured and brought to Europe by earlier explorers, had spent time in England and learned the language. He and the Wampanoag shared food with the Pilgrims, and taught them planting and fishing techniques that enabled them to survive. By 1624, Plymouth was a community of thirty small but sturdy cottages. Don't look for those simple, thatched-roof structures today – Plymouth is now a modern community of fine two-story houses, built in the latest style, where pigs and chickens no longer run in and out of the doorways.

> *"[The Indians] live at a great distance and very rarely come to the city, so that there are many inhabitants who have never seen them."*
>
> LUIGI CASTIGLIONI, AN ITALIAN VISITOR
> TO BOSTON IN THE EIGHTEENTH CENTURY

The Wampanoag were just one of many tribes that inhabited New England, all of them speakers of the Algonquian family of languages. Among them were the Pequot and Mohegan of Connecticut; the Narragansett who lived around the great bay of that name in Rhode Island; the Massachusett, who gave their name to the Bay Colony; the Pennacook of New Hampshire; the Penobscot of Maine; and, in the far north, the Abnaki, who fought on the side of the French in the recent war.

The Indian tribes of New England are led by sachems who inherit their office, like our European monarchs. Their political organization is simple – much less so than the Iroquois who live to the west, in the British colony of New York – and their lives revolve around the planting and harvest seasons, hunting and fishing, and the rituals of an animist religion with no concept of a single supreme being. To the Puritan mind, this was a religion of demon-worship, and many Congregational ministers or "divines" set about converting the Indians to Christianity. Using a Bible that had been translated into Algonquin, Reverend John Eliot established villages of "Praying Indians" in the 1660s and 1670s. Some natives were even sent to Harvard to train as ministers themselves, but only one was ever graduated.

Peace with the Indians was first broken in the Pequot War, fought in Con-

necticut in 1636 against the tribe of that name. But it was King Philip's War that broke the back of Indian resistance to white domination of New England. In 1675 and 1676, the Pokanoket sachem Metacomet (the English called him King Philip) led Nipmuc, Narragansett, and Wampanoag against the settlers, and was disastrously defeated in the "Great Swamp Fight" near Kingston, Rhode Island. From then on, New England's Indians have either lived in poor, isolated pockets within the region, or on its remote fringes.

Where can a traveler meet Indians in New England today? There is a settlement of Christianized Wampanoag on Martha's Vineyard,

Paul Revere's rendering of Metacomet (King Philip), sachem of the Pokanoket Wampanoag.

3 miles off the coast of Cape Cod, where the Indians were converted by Thomas Mayhew, Jr., son of the island's original English owner. In Natick, just west of Boston, a community of Rev. Eliot's "Praying Indians" remains, and similar groups live at Stockbridge, in the Berkshire Hills near the western border of Massachusetts, and at Mashpee, near Sandwich on Cape Cod. In Rhode Island, a few Narragansett remain on their tribal lands, although many were forced into slavery following their defeat in King Philip's War. By 1700, some 2,000 New England Indians had been enslaved, and it has been estimated that a third of the natives surviving today are slaves or menial household servants.

EARLY CONVERTS

If you'd like to meet some "Praying Indians," visit the Indian Meetinghouse in Mashpee for Sabbath Day services. The church was built in 1684, and stands alongside a burial ground with gravestones inscribed with Wampanoag names.

But the Indians have largely been driven away, to the north and west. A straggle of Penobscot and Passamaquoddy remains in the unsettled parts of Maine, and the Abnakis have retreated north from Vermont into Canada.

Still, some of our more enlightened citizens have the natives' betterment at heart. In Lebanon, Connecticut, the Reverend Eleazar Wheelock maintains a school for Christian Indians, and there is some talk of his founding a college for them, perhaps in New Hampshire, with the backing of Britain's Lord Dartmouth.

"The girls went out to service and the boys to sea, till not a soul is left."
JOHN ADAMS, LATE IN LIFE, RECALLING THE INDIANS
OF HIS HOME TOWN OF QUINCY, MASSACHUSETTS,
DURING HIS BOYHOOD IN THE 1740S

THE "GREAT MIGRATION" BEGINS

In the first decade following the founding of Salem and Boston, more than 15,000 new English settlers arrived. The flow of emigrants across the Atlantic remained vigorous throughout the 17th century and into our own, augmented by the occasional French Huguenot Protestant seeking refuge from Papist persecution at home. But unlike some of the other colonies, the population of our region remained overwhelmingly English.

ARE WE THERE YET?

Most of the early New England settlers arrived as families, often with three or more children in tow. The southern American colonies, on the other hand, were mostly settled, in their early years, by adventurous young single men.

Early seaside settlements such as Plymouth, Salem, Gloucester, Ipswich, and Boston could not contain all the new colonists, as many were farmers eager to cultivate the virgin acres of the hinterland. By 1637 the Massachusetts communities of Dorchester, Dedham, Watertown, and Concord had sprung up, each centered upon its own church. Dozens of other towns followed – and not all in Massachusetts. In 1636, Thomas Hooker and his followers left Cambridge to found Hartford, Wethersfield, and Windsor, the first English settlements in Connecticut. More momentous still, because of its religious implications, was the founding of the Rhode Island Colony in the late 1630s. The settlement at Providence dates from the expulsion of Reverend Roger Williams from Massachusetts, because of his insistence on the separation of citizenship from church membership.

By 1640, there were fledgling communities at Dover, Hampton, and Exeter, and at a place called Piscataqua, soon to be renamed Portsmouth. These and their neighboring villages north of the Merrimack River remained under Massachusetts' jurisdiction at first, but in 1679 they became part of the freshly minted royal province of New Hampshire, a quasi-autonomous dependency of Massachusetts.

Beyond these established colonies are the wilder territories of New England. The New Hampshire governor, Benning Wentworth, continues to make huge land grants along both sides of the Connecticut River, blurring the boundary between New Hampshire and the frontier country that the Reverend Samuel Peters has recently named "Verd-mont," French for "Green Mountains." Whose mountains are those? New Yorkers think they're theirs – so if you're traveling the rough pathways beyond the little town of Brattleboro, on the west bank of the Connecticut, it's best to keep your opinions on the matter to yourself until you know whether you're talking to a "Yorker" or a New Hampshireman. The odds are, though, that you will meet up instead with someone who thinks of himself simply as a Vermonter ... and they're the wrong sort to cross.

PEOPLE YOU MIGHT MEET: BENNING WENTWORTH

Governor Benning Wentworth of New Hampshire was appointed to his plum of a job by King George II in 1741. He succeeded his father, John Wentworth, in what was to become a family business – his nephew, a second John Wentworth, will take over from *him* in 1767. Benning Wentworth is a man who knows how to make a few pounds on the side while developing his colony: he's busy carving some 124 new townships out of the New Hampshire wilderness, making sure he reserves 500 acres or more from each town for himself. His landholdings will eventually total 100,000 acres, all of it sure to appreciate in value as the colony grows and prospers. If you're for-

Governor Benning Wentworth.

tunate, you might be invited to visit the governor at his splendid Portsmouth mansion, where the portly old gentleman serves fine Madeira from crystal decanters to the seaport's upper crust.

"An unbroken wilderness ... Till the commencement of the French war a large proportion of this region was little known to civilized men, few of whom had ever penetrated its sequestered recesses."

FROM AN EARLY HISTORY OF THE TOWN OF PITTSFORD, VERMONT

TROUBLES WITH THE BRITISH CROWN

As the New England colonies grew and began to prosper, Great Britain left them pretty much alone. Their original charters, after all, gave them plenty of leeway to manage their own affairs. Towns handled local issues in meetings attended by male landholders (who, in the early days, had to be church members), and sent representatives to colonial legislatures such as Massachusetts' Great and General Court. All went well during the eleven years of Britain's Puritan Commonwealth under Oliver Cromwell, and through-out the reign of Charles II after the monarchy had been restored. But in 1686, King James II tried to tighten the mother country's hold on her colonies by revoking the New England and middle Atlantic colonies' charters, and appointing a royal governor to rule over a "Dominion of New England in America." Today's traveler in these colonies can well imagine how happily this scheme was received, especially given the current growing resentment against royal power. Sir Edmund Andros, the tyrant King James appointed as governor, was dragged from the Massachusetts State House and clapped in irons as soon as word arrived that James himself had been booted off the throne in the "Glorious Revolution" of 1688. Governors appointed in London still sit in New England's capitals, but the real work of local government is back in the hands of our legislatures and town meetings.

Sir Edmund Andros, despised New England governor.

THE FRENCH THREAT ENDED

Of course, New Englanders are pleased to have London's help when facing a foreign foe. The recent war with the French was just such an occasion. It was part of a larger struggle between Britain and France, and in Europe they called it the Seven Years' War – but in the colonies, it was all about escaping the threat from Catholic New France and its Indian allies that had hung over New England from the earliest days of settlement. Nowhere did that menace strike more fiercely than in the Connecticut River valley town of Deerfield, Massachusetts, where in 1704 an Abnaki raid instigated by the French took the lives

New France's capital of Quebec falls to General Wolfe's British forces, 1759.

of about fifty townspeople. A hundred more were carried off to captivity in Quebec. If your travels take you as far as Springfield, it's worth a day's ride north along the pretty valley to see the scars the little village still bears. On the door of one house, you can run your hand across the gashes made by an Indian's tomahawk as a family cowered inside.

But now French rule in North America is finished. In 1758 the British routed the French from their great fortress at Louisbourg, in Nova Scotia, with the help of brave Massachusetts militiamen. Meanwhile, in the west, British regulars and Virginians swept the French from the Ohio valley; one hears that an especially able young officer named George Washington gave an excellent account of himself in this campaign. Finally, Quebec itself fell, in 1759, and Montreal was taken the following year.

Prying the French from their strongholds was a costly business. New England's economy has yet to recover, and few of its citizens are comfortable with having so many British soldiers among them. And everyone is concerned over Britain's war debts, and how deep she will have to dig into colonial pockets to repay them. Already there are rumors of new taxes, of levies on sugar and silk and wine; will tea be next?

~~~

"I have been told by Englishmen … that the English colonies in North America, in the space of thirty, forty, or fifty years, would be able to form a state by themselves, entirely independent of Old England."

PETER KALM, *SOURCES OF AMERICAN NATIONALITY*, 1753–61

~~~

A MORE SECULAR SOCIETY

The New England of the 1760s is still a God-fearing place, although it no longer exists solely to be the new Zion envisioned by its founders. And it no longer subscribes only to the Puritan faith – one of the handsomest new buildings in Boston, in fact, is the Church of England's King's Chapel, built of Quincy granite and standing near the Common. The "Great Awakening" evangelists of the 1740s have led many to the new Baptist sect, and there is even a Jewish community, with its own synagogue, in Newport, Rhode Island. But what you won't find in these colonies is a congregation of Roman Catholics.

Interior of King's Chapel, Boston's first Anglican house of worship.

PAPIST INROAD

The first Catholic Mass in Boston would not be celebrated until 1778.
The occasion was the funeral of a French naval officer killed in
a bread riot, and buried at King's Chapel.

It's no longer necessary to be a church communicant to vote at town meetings, and the colonies aren't likely to see further episodes such as the seventeenth-century hanging of Quakers on Boston Common, or the Salem witch trials of the 1690s, which resulted in more than 20 citizens being executed for consorting with the Devil (we'll take a closer look at this strange and tragic episode when we visit that Massachusetts town in Chapter Five of this guide). Old-school Congregational ministers may warn that New Englanders are going soft, and that they care more about making money – and perhaps having their portraits painted by Copley and their gowns imported from England – than they do about salvation. But to most colonists, the hammering of our shipbuilders and housewrights, the diligence of our farmers, artisans, and merchants, and the clamor of trade upon our docks is proof aplenty that we have made, if not a new Zion, a New England in the New World.

III

THE LAY OF THE LAND

I f you were headed for Virginia, New England in the middle of November might seem something of a disappointment. That was the situation the Pilgrims found themselves in, when they landed at the tip of Cape Cod, where the fishing village of Provincetown now stands, in 1620. (Plymouth was actually their second stop, after they realized that those bleak outer reaches of the Cape were undersupplied with fresh water and oversupplied, in their view, with hostile Indians.)

Plymouth certainly wasn't Virginia – not in climate, nor in terrain. But the Pilgrims, and the settlers that followed them, found a landscape that in many places wasn't at all unlike the Britain they had left behind. We're talking, of course, about spring and summertime New England, not the New England that's covered with snow for nearly six months of the year.

It did take a century and a half of hard work to get parts of New England looking like an English shire. The first colonists found dense forests of maple, birch, and beech in the southern lowlands, and spruce, fir, and pine farther north. Those tall pines have always been valued by the British navy for ships' masts, and it's still against the law to cut them down for any other use. If you like it here and plan to stay and build a house, don't get caught with floorboards wider than 23 inches. Trees more than 2 feet in diameter are the King's pines, marked by surveyors with the broad arrow insignia of the Royal Navy.

~~~

"The next commodity the land affords, is a good store of woods,
& that not only such as may be needful for fuel, but likewise for
the building of ships, and houses, & mills, and for all manner
of waterwork about which wood is needful."
WILLIAM WOOD, *NEW ENGLAND'S PROSPECTS*, 1634

~~~

A VITAL HARVEST

"Mast trees," as they're called, are felled in the fall, and hauled over snow in winter by teams of dozens of oxen. They're gathered at mast landings, where they're loaded onto specially built ships bound for British dockyards.

The vast New England forests, which grew even in the sandy soil of Cape Cod and the islands of Nantucket and Martha's Vineyard, began falling to settlers' axes as soon as the first ships landed. What good are forests, except for timber to build with, and to make charcoal for smelting metals? Indians might hide in the dark woods, and to our Puritan ancestors, they were the abode of demons. Besides, many of those first British New Englanders were farmers, eager to clear land for cultivation.

Our neighbors to the south – especially those rich tobacco planters of Maryland and Virginia – might joke that tilling any of New England's stony acres is a fool's business. But this is how these colonies were settled, by men with axes, and with oxen for pulling stumps, claiming farmland from the wilderness inch by inch, mile by mile, until the coastal lowlands and the river valleys got their settled, English look.

"To clear a farm covered with a thick growth of large trees such as generally abound in this country is a work of no small magnitude. Especially is this true when, as is usually the fact, it is to be done by a single man."

TIMOTHY DWIGHT, *TRAVELS IN NEW ENGLAND AND NEW YORK*, 1822

SALT AND FRESH WATER

The coastline of New England offers a wealth of natural harbors. The greatest of these is Boston harbor, protected by a cluster of islands at the head of Massachusetts Bay, where the Mystic and the Charles rivers meet, in the words of some proud local wags, "to form the Atlantic Ocean." Newport and Providence are the great harbors of Rhode Island, in Narragansett Bay, and the shipyards and warehouses of Portsmouth cluster about the mouth of the Piscataqua River, dividing New Hampshire from Maine. Farther north stretches the fantastically ragged and rocky coast of Maine itself, where settlements are sparse – but where harbors lie close to fine stands of timber for shipbuilding, and for shipment as firewood for Massachusetts hearths.

New England is amply threaded with rivers. The Kennebec and Penobscot rush down from the wild interior of Maine, and the swift Merrimack descends from New Hampshire's mountains to meet the Atlantic at the shipyards of Newburyport. Greatest of all is the Connecticut, which flows from the border with Canada to tidewater at Long Island Sound. The Connecticut River is proving to be a great highway of settlement, as

Detail from a 1768 Paul Revere engraving showing Boston's North End and Mill Pond.

A French map of the New England and Middle Atlantic colonies, 1757.

farmers seeking new land travel north from Connecticut and Massachusetts to the far reaches of Vermont and New Hampshire. Already, settlers in the upper Connecticut valley townships granted by New Hampshire's governor, Benning Wentworth, have begun to name their fledgling villages after the communities they left behind – Springfield, Hartford, and Lebanon are just a few examples. When it comes to naming towns, New Englanders are not creatures of great imagination: they brought English names across the ocean, and carried Connecticut and Massachusetts names upriver.

New England rivers are working rivers. Along nearly every stream, at the head of navigation, you'll find a waterwheel turning the machinery of a mill. Our mills grind grain, like the mills back in Europe, but here water power is also put to use in sawing timber into boards. The water-powered sawmill, with its up-and-down blade, is a purely American invention. With all our water and all our wood, it didn't take long after the colonists first arrived before "Yankee ingenuity" – as some are beginning to call it – found a way to bring the two together. There are even those who think that waterwheels can set looms to clattering, and weave cloth, but this may be an idle dream. There's only so much ingenuity, even in a Yankee.

MOUNTAINS OF NORTHERN NEW ENGLAND

There are fearsome barriers to settlement in much of northern New England, even now that the French and the Abnaki have been vanquished. Far in the northern reaches of New Hampshire are mountains whose summits are not only treeless, but without even a covering of soil. The Indians call the loftiest of these Agiocochook, and it stands so tall that it can be seen from ships at sea, more than 80 miles distant. Captain John Smith, sailing along our shores in 1614, recorded it as "the twinkling mountain," so bright did its rocky peak shine in the sunlight. For no good reason – why climb such a mountain? – an Englishman named Darby Field made his way to the top as long ago as 1642. His Indian guides deserted him along the way, believing that the summit was the realm of spirits. It may as well have been, because few travelers have followed in his footsteps in all the years since. By no means can the editors of this guide vouch for the safety of anyone foolish enough to attempt this climb today. Even if there are no Indian spirits, that barren mountaintop is said to be the abode of winds that can blow a man clear to Casco Bay, on the coast of Maine.

HIS ORIGINAL MONUMENT

After the American Revolution, the Indians' Agiocochook
would be renamed Mount Washington.

The Green Mountains of Vermont are less daunting than those White Hills of New Hampshire, but they are heavily wooded, as their name might suggest, and they have been only very sparsely settled. We mentioned earlier that this rugged country was still under a cloud of uncertainty as to just who it belongs to – New Hampshire, or New York? – but even if the tangle of competing claims is ever resolved, it's unlikely that such miserable terrain for cultivation will ever attract many settlers. An exception might be the bottomlands along Lake Champlain, which may prove as useful a water highway for peaceable commerce, as it was an avenue of conquest for the Iroquois, for the French, and for our forces in the late war. Still, it's hard to imagine that a splendid natural fortress site like that at Ticonderoga, on Champlain's New York shore, has left behind its days of military usefulness.

Settlers trek north along the Connecticut River, into the wilds of Vermont.

JUST WHAT DID HE SAY?

Sure enough, Fort Ticonderoga would again make history: in 1775, Ethan Allen and his Green Mountain Boys took the stronghold in a dawn raid, with Allen allegedly ordering the British commander to surrender "in the name of Jehovah and the Continental Congress." Other accounts have Allen demanding, "Come out of there, you damned rat."

Ethan Allen and his Green Mountain Boys plot a raid.

A NEW ENGLAND BESTIARY

If you're traveling in the more settled parts of New England, you won't have much to fear from wild animals. Bears and wolves have disappeared along with the trees from the farmlands of Massachusetts, Rhode Island, and Connecticut. But in the forests of northern New England, these beasts as well as the fierce panther or catamount, a cat as large as a grown man, still roam freely. Among other denizens of the great woods are deer that grow larger than the European roe and fallow deer; the great ungainly moose; the lynx and bobcat; and two creatures that travelers would be wise to avoid, the porcupine and the skunk. The first is a relative of the European hedgehog, but larger, and can release his painful quills into an intruder's flesh with a lash of his tail. The Indians dye these quills, and weave them into colorful designs on boxes, bags, and moccasins

The porcupine, an animal best avoided.

(see Chapter Eight). As for the skunk, there is nothing like him in Britain or continental Europe. Pester a skunk and let him spray his stink upon your clothes, and your innkeeper will make you sleep in the stable – if the horses can stand the smell of you.

The moose, largest member of the deer family, roams New England's forests.

All in all, New England wouldn't be anyone's first choice as a promising place to settle, except perhaps for fishermen who planned to turn their backs on those thick forests and spend their days harvesting what seems to be an endless supply of codfish on the Grand Banks. The soils are mostly poor, and the ground coughs up so many rocks that a Yankee farmer's first great crop is the stone walls that snake across our landscape everywhere you look. Once you get away from the coast and the river valleys, you'll have a hard time finding level ground, and there are plenty of places where, according to a popular jest, it's so hilly that the farmers raise a special breed of cow with legs shorter on one side than the other. But the difficult New England terrain has proven to be a good place for raising one useful and indispensable thing: New Englanders.

IV

MEET THE NEW ENGLANDERS

~~~

*"The American is a new man, who acts upon new principles; he must
therefore entertain new ideas, and form new opinions."*

MICHEL-GUILLAUME JEAN (J. HECTOR ST. JOHN) DE CRÈVECOEUR,
LETTERS FROM AN AMERICAN FARMER, 1783

~~~

New Englanders are farmers, artisans, merchants, preachers, housewrights, blacksmiths, shipbuilders, fishermen – all of the things they
might have been in the Old World. New England never saw much of
a migration of either the very rich or the very poor to its shores. The people
you'll meet here are mostly drawn from the English middle classes, although
some families, of course, have fared better than others since their arrival.

Ninety-five percent of New England's population is of English descent.
Here you won't find the great number of Dutchmen and Germans who live in
New York and Pennsylvania, the Swedes of Delaware and New Jersey, nor even
the Scotch-Irish that are beginning to settle the southern Appalachian hinterlands. As we mentioned in Chapter Two, most New Englanders don't even
descend from a very wide sampling of English stock, coming as they did – and
still do – from Dorset, Lincolnshire, and East Anglia.

If you're English yourself and are coming to New England to sample an
exotic culture, then you're coming to the wrong place. But look beneath the
surface – get to know people of city and town – and you will find another sort
of citizen than you're used to at home. A southern planter, or even a New
Yorker, will also get the sense that people are just a little different here.

From the days of their earliest arrival, New Englanders have been creatures
of their towns. To be sure, a Massachusetts man will identify himself as such,
and the same is true of the other colonies as well. But he will likely, first and
foremost, see himself as a Medford man, or a citizen of Cohasset or Newbury,
Andover or Middleborough. This is where his ancestors carved out their farms,

Town meetings are seldom as contentious as in this John Trumbull engraving.

where they built their church – and in those days town and church, remember, were all but one. The town meeting is the cornerstone of their political life, the town militia the pillar of their defense. We have our colonial governors, and our legislatures that meet in each colony's capital – Boston in Massachusetts,

Portsmouth in New Hampshire, Hartford in Connecticut, and various places in Rhode Island. But New England is really a constellation of towns.

Each taxpaying citizen, in each of those towns, feels a proprietary interest in the place, and doesn't hesitate to make his opinions and grievances known at town meeting. In a city such as Boston, of course, there will be more of a merchant aristocracy, comfortable at the governor's table, as well as a greater number of poor and propertyless laborers and mechanics. Merchant, shopkeeper, and laborer alike will suffer when the economic depression of 1765 hits hard, when banks fail and only a fifth as many ships as usual sail to trade with the West Indies. Here, grievance against Parliament and the Crown will more likely be voiced in the streets, as will happen when the Stamp Act threatens in that same year to post a duty on documents ranging from newspapers to legal papers; or in the courts, as when James Otis had his say against the Writs of Assistance in 1761. But in the small towns, everything revolves around the meetinghouse.

PEOPLE YOU MIGHT MEET: JAMES OTIS

James Otis is believed by many Bostonians to be the best lawyer in the city. By his mid-thirties, this big, moody, quick-tempered barrister had risen to the post of King's Advocate. But he resigned from this prestigious post

in order to represent a coalition of Boston merchants petitioning against the "Writs of Assistance," documents authorized by Parliament that allowed customs officials to enter – by force if necessary – any ship, warehouse, or even private home to secure evidence in tax cases. Not that Otis cares to see the colonies slough off London's rule altogether: he's on record for saying that the British Empire is "best calculated for general happiness of any that has yet risen to view in the world," and that an America independent of Britain would be something that only "rebels, fools,

Copley's portrait of James Otis.

[and] madmen will contend for." Ironically, Otis will come to fill two of those roles – as an orator and pamphleteer increasingly at odds with British policy; and as a man who descends into insanity as the result of a blow from a customs official's cutlass during a coffeehouse fracas.

PEOPLE YOU MIGHT MEET: JOHN HANCOCK

One of Boston's young men to watch is John Hancock, who stands to inherit the estate of his aging uncle, Thomas Hancock, the most prominent merchant and wealthiest man in New England. Now in his early twenties, Hancock is a thin, handsome fellow, a vain clotheshorse who can talk a blue streak. Whether he is all chatter, or turns out to be capable of holding on to the £70,000 his uncle is said to be worth, is all that concerns most Boston gossips – but he will be remembered less for his inherited fortune than for his massively ornate signature on the Declaration of Independence, and his subsequent service as governor of the state – not the colony – of Massachusetts.

Paul Revere engraving of John Hancock.

These colonies also have a wild frontier, and wild frontiersmen to go along with it. An even more independent species of New Englander inhabits the far reaches of northern New Hampshire, Maine, and Vermont. The farther you travel from the earliest settled areas along the seacoast and the river valleys, the less definite the borders, and the more these pioneers must improvise their land and legal arrangements. And "legal" is often a laughably imprecise term, especially when the subject at hand is that interminable wrangle between New Hampshire and New York over the mountainous wastes that lie between them. As we've already noted, it takes a rough brand of men to colonize such places.

NEW ENGLAND'S DISTAFF SIDE

One thing that might surprise you, as you travel in New England, is that women hold a stronger position in society than in Britain, or even in other parts of the American colonies. Don't be alarmed – they certainly aren't equal with men under the law – but given the hardships of setting up communities, households, and farms in early colonial times, women often found themselves with greater responsibilities, and haven't been inclined to give them up. (Life was hard for the early southern colonists, too, but they didn't include all that many women among their numbers.)

PEOPLE YOU MIGHT MEET: TWO MEN NAMED ADAMS

Boston's tax collector is a feckless fellow in his late thirties named Samuel Adams. He once had good prospects as proprietor of the brewery inher-

ited from his father, old Deacon Adams; he made a decent enough beer but was so careless with figures that he soon enough lost the business. What talent he does have is for endless talk of politics – but of all the offices he might have talked Boston voters into giving him, tax collector is the one for which he is least suited. He has such an ear for the sad stories of the poor that he collects nothing at all from them. It's hard to imagine that he will come to anything but a bad end, haranguing anyone who will listen in the taverns, and drinking other men's beer instead of his own. But he will emerge as one of the firebrands of the American Revolution, a prime instigator of the 1773 Boston Tea Party, and governor of Massachusetts after independence.

Copley's portrait of Samuel Adams.

John Adams grew up on his father's farm in Quincy, a Massachusetts town south of Boston. He was graduated from Harvard College, and took to the

law. He was admitted to the bar in 1759, having studied under a prominent attorney in Worcester, Massachusetts. Although he recently lost his first case, he has written that he hopes to become "a great man," unlike "the common herd of mankind." But in pursuing his dream, he vows "never to commit any meanness or injustice in the practice of law." John Adams will stick to his ideals of justice, even defending the British soldiers accused in the Boston Massacre of 1770. He will also serve as a delegate to the Continental Congress, sign the Declaration of Independence, and be elected second president of the United States.

A portrait of John Adams by Benjamin Blyth.

"On the road you often come upon those fair Connecticut girls driving a carriage or galloping boldly alone on horseback and wearing fine hats, white aprons, and calico gowns. Such encounters prove the early cultivation of their intellect, since they are trusted so young by themselves. They also reflect the safety of the roads and the general innocence of manners. You will see maidens hazarding themselves alone without protectors in the public stagecoaches. I am wrong to say hazarding. Who can offend them?"

JEAN PIERRE BRISSOT, *A NEW VOYAGE TO THE UNITED STATES*, 1791

Women aren't entitled to vote in New England, nor own or inherit property, unless they are widows, but they are generally allowed to cast votes on behalf of their families if their husbands are unable to report to town meeting – something that must often have been the case during the recent war against the French and Indians. They are accepted as church members, often in greater numbers than their husbands, but of course they do not preach. At home, though, they are the ones you will find at fireside, teaching their children the Scriptures. And the midwife is a necessary and respected member of each community.

Copley's portrait of Mrs. Samuel Waldo, née Griselda Oliver, Boston society woman.

Stop at any inn along your journeys through New England, and alongside your landlord you are likely to find a hardworking landlady, who considers herself as much a proprietor of the establishment as her husband. Except for the humblest servant girls, and the ladies of the loftiest royal officials (who must, after all, have their husbands' ears), the women of New England are partners, often unsung but always at hand, in the running of our colonial society.

THE SCANDAL OF SIR HARRY FRANKLAND

Not so long ago – in 1742 – young Sir Harry Frankland was customs collector of the port of Boston. One afternoon, while traveling north of the city on business, he paused for a tankard of beer at the Fountain Inn in Marblehead. It was there that he became hopelessly smitten with a barefoot serving girl, Agnes Surriage, the sixteen-year-old daughter of a local fisherman. On his next visit to Marblehead, Sir Harry asked, and received, permission to bring the girl to Boston as his ward, and to oversee her education.

Sir Harry kept his part of the bargain, and as Agnes stayed closely in touch with her mother and her minister, the tongues of Boston gossips were kept temporarily in check. But after the girl's father died, and she became a permanent part of his household, the rumors began to fly. Sir Harry, recently made a baronet, of course could not marry below his station – but neither did he care to put up with the disapproving stares of Boston society. He and Agnes left town for Hopkinton, Massachusetts, some 25 miles distant, where Sir Harry built Frankland Hall. The pair lived there happily and in 1754 took a trip to his ancestral home in England, and from there to the continent. While visiting Lisbon in the following year, Sir Harry was nearly killed in the great earthquake which destroyed the city, and was rescued by Agnes. The event chastened him – and today Agnes Surriage, the Marblehead tavern girl, is Lady Frankland. The couple came back to Boston in 1756, left a year later, and returned briefly in 1763. They currently reside in England.

AFRICANS IN NEW ENGLAND

There is a black African presence in New England, consisting of both slaves and freemen. The soil in these colonies is hardly rich enough to allow the setting up of vast plantations, as in the south, and so there has never been a call for slavery on a large scale. The great majority of New Englanders have never been slaveholders at all – the greatest number are in Connecticut, where perhaps they amount to a quarter of all families – and those who do keep slaves rarely have more than one or two, who are usually employed in farm labor or household service (to this day, enslaved Indians also add to these numbers). Ministers, physicians, prosperous merchants, and wealthy farmers are their likely masters, as small New England landholders have enough trouble feeding their own families, without having to care for slaves as well.

EARLY ABOLITIONISTS

Slavery will become extremely uncommon in New England as the 18th century draws to a close. In 1777, Vermont's constitution as an independent republic will ban the practice outright – the first American state, or future state, to do so.

Black freemen live in all of New England's cities and larger towns, where they mostly take the same employment as the laboring classes of whites. It's estimated that one in ten citizens of Boston are of African descent – their numbers are concentrated along the back slope of the Trimount – and in Newport, Rhode Island, they represent a quarter of the populace.

A recent development among black New Englanders is the celebration of "'Lection Day," held on the same day as town and colony elections. More than just a mocking of enfranchised citizens' voting, the 'Lection Day activities actually involve the casting of votes for informal leaders with real authority within the African communities, and are always marked with celebrations and parades.

INDENTURES AND APPRENTICES

While not nearly as common as it is in the middle Atlantic and southern colonies, the system of indentured servitude has brought a number of settlers to New England. Although other arrangements are sometimes made, indenture usually entails the selling of one's services to a master for a period of time sufficient to pay the cost of passage from Britain or continental Europe (in New York and Pennsylvania, a large number of Germans arrive in this way).

New England is a place where a man and his family can rise above their class with greater ease than in the Old World, and little prejudice is held against individuals who worked their way up from indenture. You may meet some of them in your travels, and never be aware of their humble origins.

Indenture is different from apprenticeship, which is how so many of our New England artisans learn their trades. As in Britain and other nations, young men who desire to rise in the world (or whose parents wish to see to it that they rise, or else) are put in the employ of masters at various crafts, who agree to teach and board them in return for their labor. Admire an exquisite chocolate-pot, or a fine piece of cabinetry, and you are doubtless enjoying the work of a one-time apprentice.

"Indentured servants are preferable to all others, because they are not so expensive [as slaves] … and men or maids who get yearly wages are likewise too costly. But this kind of servant can be gotten for half the money, and even less."

PETER KALM, *A JOURNEY TO NORTH AMERICA*, 1753–61

All in all, it's safe to say that New Englanders are a people of proud and independent spirit, men and women who think they are no one's inferiors. Perhaps this is because their forebears were hard-minded religious dissenters, who in their homeland overthrew a king, and who came to these shores to create a godly realm where compromise was out of the question. Perhaps it has to do with having lived, this past century and a half, so far from a place where privilege and social standing are unassailable. But most likely of all, it's because of their immense pride and satisfaction in having built so sturdy a set of colonies, in spite of fearsome weather, hostile natives, and a hard and stony soil.

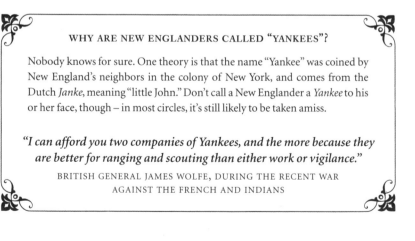

WHY ARE NEW ENGLANDERS CALLED "YANKEES"?

Nobody knows for sure. One theory is that the name "Yankee" was coined by New England's neighbors in the colony of New York, and comes from the Dutch *Janke*, meaning "little John." Don't call a New Englander a *Yankee* to his or her face, though – in most circles, it's still likely to be taken amiss.

"I can afford you two companies of Yankees, and the more because they are better for ranging and scouting than either work or vigilance."

BRITISH GENERAL JAMES WOLFE, DURING THE RECENT WAR AGAINST THE FRENCH AND INDIANS

V

TRAVELING WITHIN NEW ENGLAND

Once you've arrived in New England, you'll want to explore beyond the confines of the city where your ship has docked – Boston, most probably, but perhaps Portsmouth or Newport. Your choices for travel are simple: you'll go overland, or, if your destination is along the coast, by water. Traveling by ship is often preferred by New Englanders heading to Boston's great rival as a port city, New York – but it's not without its dangers. Sailing south from Newport or New Haven on the calm waters of Long Island Sound is easy. But leaving Boston, your ship will have to round Cape Cod, with its dangerous shoals. To make things worse, certain rogues along the Cape's wild shore have turned to lighting false beacons and luring ships to their doom, so they may murder sailors and passengers and plunder the wrecks. These brigands have earned the name of "mooncussers," since they work their mischief best on dark nights and curse the moon for betraying them. As long ago as 1623, the Pilgrim Captain Myles Standish ventured a plan for digging a canal that would cut the great arm of the cape off at the shoulder, shortening the distance from northern New England to points south – but where would we ever find enough men to shovel so much earth? For now and likely forever, we'll have to round the cape under sail. But we hope to build a good many more lighthouses like our fine Boston Light.

Of course, there are only so many places a traveler can reach by water – although on our great rivers, like the Connecticut, flat-bottomed boats carry both passengers and goods north from

Hartford to Springfield. But don't expect a stateroom. You'll pass your days on deck, and your nights like the boatmen do, in taverns along the route.

A DAINTY CAPE COD DINNER

If you do end up in the sandy, desolate wilds of Cape Cod, in the hands of an honest householder rather than the mooncussers, beware of what might be on the evening menu. Cape Codders are so poor that they're known to eat seagulls, an abundant but most unpalatable bird, which they catch by digging pits in the sand, covering them with brush baited with dead fish, and lurking below so they can grab the gulls by the feet when they alight for their meal.

New England's roads are better than they once were, but in many places that isn't saying very much. They began with trails used by the Indians and were widened enough to make way for men on horseback, and later wagons and carriages. The best of them link the largest cities and towns, where the traffic is greatest and the post must be carried as swiftly as possible.

Even on the best roads, if you're traveling by coach, expect to proceed at a speed of about 4 or 5 miles an hour, with extra time built in for a change of

Late eighteenth-century stagecoach, typical of conveyances used on main roads.

horses every 10 miles or so. And figure on stopping at a tavern or inn around noon. That's when to expect dinner, the principal meal of the day. Your coachman will sound his horn as he approaches this welcome resting place, to let the landlord know that hungry travelers are arriving.

～✧～

"Ducks, ham, chickens, beef, pig, tarts, creams, custards, jellies, fools, trifles, floating islands, beer, porter, punch, wine ... "

FROM A DESCRIPTION BY JOHN ADAMS OF A PARTICULARLY
LUXURIOUS SPREAD LAID OUT FOR DINNER AT A STAGECOACH STOP.
WE CAN ONLY ASSUME HE WAS PATRONIZING ONE OF THE BETTER
ESTABLISHMENTS, ALONG A VERY WELL-TRAVELED ROUTE

～✧～

The dinner stop will be a welcome one indeed. Your stagecoach might start out as early as three o'clock in the morning, especially in summer when the sun rises early, and a day's journey might last sixteen or seventeen hours. "Fine," you might say. "What sleep I don't get in bed at night, I'll catch while on the road." Good luck to you: aside from being cramped among your fellow passengers, and jostling over every bump along the way, you'll have to deal with clouds of dust if the windows of your conveyance are open, and intolerable heat if its curtains are drawn. "It's a comfort," one stage passenger remarked not long ago, "to shift one's position and be bruised in a new place."

All discomfort aside, there is one thing that a visitor to these shores need not worry about when traveling by coach. Unlike British stage routes, those in New England are not bedeviled by highwaymen. You might think yourself robbed by an innkeeper whose bed and board doesn't measure up to your standards, but your stage won't be stopped and your pocket picked by those dry-land pirates.

～✧～

"[In the Middle and New England colonies people usually traveled in winter in sleighs standing] upon two pieces of wood that lye flat on the ground like a North of England sled, the forepart turning up with a bent to slide over stones or any little rising and shod with smooth plates of iron to prevent their wearing away too fast."

BRITISH TRAVELER JAMES BIRKET, 1750

～✧～

VISITING BOSTON AND ENVIRONS

Boston is the great metropolis of New England, its principal port and seat of culture. It is a city of wharves (forty, at last count), warehouses, ropewalks, ships' chandlers, and the busy shops of artisans and the sellers of fine and necessary goods; and it is of course the seat of Massachusetts' colonial government. It boasts a population of nearly 16,000 souls and is the third largest city in British North America after Philadelphia and New York.

As we noted earlier, Boston was built upon the oddly-shaped Shawmut Peninsula, almost an island save for "The Neck," a mere thread of land that links it to Roxbury on the mainland. The city proper jams itself onto the peninsula, which juts between the mouth of the Charles River and the great natural harbor at the head of Massachusetts Bay; its principal suburbs are

GETTING AWAY FROM IT ALL

Roxbury is a favorite rural retreat of prominent Bostonians. Perhaps the most impressive of the homes that the powerful and well-to-do have built in this country setting is the mansion of former Massachusetts Governor William Shirley. Designed by talented architect Peter Harrison, Governor Shirley's classically proportioned house is the centerpiece of a 33-acre estate, and is surrounded with beautiful landscaped gardens.

William Shirley, who is at present royal governor of the Bahamas, served Massachusetts with distinction both as governor (1741–49 and 1753–56), and as a military strategist. He set the finances of the colony on a sound footing, and was largely responsible for planning the 1745 attack that drove the French from their fortress at Louisbourg in Nova Scotia. When his service in the Bahamas is concluded, Bostonians expect that he will retire to his Roxbury estate to live out his days. (Governor Shirley did indeed return to Roxbury in 1770, although his retirement was cut short by his death, at seventy-six, less than a year later.)

Governor Shirley's country mansion.

Charlestown, north across the Charles, and Cambridge, also on the other side of that brackish stream and several miles to the west. The village of Roxbury, like Dorchester, lies on the mainland side of the neck and somewhat to the south.

Boston's Trimount (Beacon Hill, center), as it appeared to the first settlers.

The only land approach to Boston, then, is by way of The Neck, and here stands the town gate, a brick structure that is always manned by sentries. Passing through the gate, a traveler will arrive on High Street, which continues into the heart of the city while changing its name, as it proceeds, from Orange to Newbury to Marlborough, and finally to Cornhill. To the west lies the Common, where Bostonians grazed their animals in the earliest days of settlement. It is a grassy, open space, used at times as a militia training ground, and more often by idle boys as a place to frolic, catch frogs, and pick blueberries. On a grimmer note, it is where criminals are hung, from an ancient oak, and one corner of the Common is the site of a burying ground. (Boston's other graveyards are on Copp's Hill in North Boston; alongside King's Chapel; and at a spot just east of the Common called the Granary, after a grain storage building which once stood nearby.)

Just beyond the Common, to the north, rise the three steep summits of the Trimount, the loftiest being Beacon Hill, so named for the pot of pitch set ablaze there in the century past as a guiding light for ships approaching the harbor. The lesser western summit, Mount Vernon, has acquired the name "Mount Whoredom" for the scandalous reputation of the neighborhood that straggles down its northern slope; and some say that the name of its district's

Joy Street reflects the same character. On the respectable side of the hill, though, the elegant mansion of merchant Thomas Hancock bespeaks no vice save simple acquisitiveness.

Beyond the Common and the hilltops the Shawmut Peninsula narrows again, hemmed in by the harbor to the east and the Mill Pond to the north. The Mill Pond, dammed across its northern outlet at the Charles, has become a vile and malodorous pool, where butchers and candle makers dump their offal, and we would not be in the least surprised if it is someday filled in to make land for the growing city. Its eastern fringe touches the final widening of the peninsula, the old district called North Boston, where twisting little lanes recall the cramped haphazard settlement that followed the arrival of John Winthrop and his fellow emigrants aboard the *Arbella*, nearly a century and a half ago.

All along their watery fringe, North Boston and the neighborhoods to the south are lined with wharves. The most impressive of these is Long Wharf, which runs a half mile out into the island-strewn harbor. Long Wharf is really a continuation of King Street, the broad, short thoroughfare that begins at the front door of the Massachusetts State House.

Seat of Government

The State House has been the seat of the colony's government since 1713. It is a fine brick building with a step-gabled façade, and on opposite sides of the balcony facing King Street are carved, brightly painted representations of those ancient symbols of British royal authority, the lion and the unicorn.

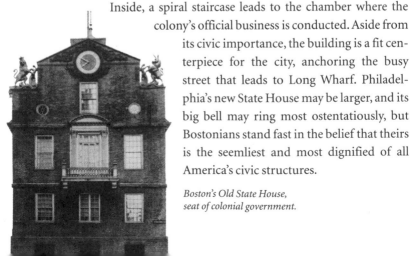

Inside, a spiral staircase leads to the chamber where the colony's official business is conducted. Aside from its civic importance, the building is a fit centerpiece for the city, anchoring the busy street that leads to Long Wharf. Philadelphia's new State House may be larger, and its big bell may ring most ostentatiously, but Bostonians stand fast in the belief that theirs is the seemliest and most dignified of all America's civic structures.

Boston's Old State House, seat of colonial government.

A TALE OF TWO STATE HOUSES

Later known as the "Old State House," the old colonial administration building would be replaced by Charles Bulfinch's magnificent new State House, begun in 1795 on the truncated summit of Beacon Hill. The old structure served for a while as Boston City Hall, then fell nearly into dereliction prior to its restoration in the 1880s. The lion and unicorn, pulled down during the Revolution (they had looked directly down on the Boston Massacre, in 1770) were replaced with replicas that flanked Queen Elizabeth II during her address from the balcony during a 1976 visit to celebrate the American bicentennial.

And Pennsylvania's State House? It was soon to become known as Independence Hall, and its great bell entered history as the Liberty Bell.

A Pair of Impressive Churches

At Cornhill and Milk streets, a scant two blocks from the State House, stands the Old South Meeting House, solidly built of brick, dating to 1729. It is the largest edifice in Boston – so large, in fact, that it is used for citizens' meetings that cannot fit into Faneuil Hall (see below), the usual place for civic gatherings. Old South – it still carries the name "meeting-house," favored for places of worship by the Puritan Congregationalists who built its wooden predecessor in the early days of Boston – is one of the first signs of Boston a passenger on an arriving ship will see, as its lovely white steeple rises 183 feet above Cornhill.

Boston's Anglican Christ Church. Its magnificent steeple rises more than 190 feet.

Up on Salem Street in North Boston, Christ Church has stood six years longer than the Old South, and its steeple reaches some 8 feet higher. Like King's Chapel – of which more in Chapter Seven – Christ Church is staunchly

Anglican, and after King's was the second place of worship to challenge the old Puritan dominance in Boston. Not surprisingly, given its Church of England affiliation, Christ's congregation represents the more affluent and staunchly loyalist portion of the city's population, and no service held here omits the traditional prayers for the health and safety of the King. King George III, in fact, was the donor of the church's exquisite communion silver. The elegant interior and upper-class associations of Christ Church evidently have their appeal even to good young Congregationalists: when he was a boy of fifteen, the silversmith Paul Revere took employment as one of the ringers of Christ's "royal peal" of eight sonorous bells.

"We are the first ring of bells cast for the British Empire in North America."

1744 INSCRIPTION ON ONE OF THE BELLS OF CHRIST CHURCH, BOSTON

THE CHURCHES' REVOLUTIONARY ROLE

The Old South Meeting House will be the gathering place for irate colonists who, galvanized by Samuel Adams' fiery words, head for the harbor and stage the Boston Tea Party in December, 1773. And from the steeple of Christ Church, later known informally as Old North, the signal lanterns of Paul Revere will shine on the night of April 18, 1775.

A Generous Bequest

Faneuil Hall, which stands near the waterfront just north of King Street, is Boston's town meeting place. It was built in 1742, the gift of merchant Peter Faneuil, and was designed by a Scottish emigrant to Boston named John Smibert, who was far better known as a portrait painter than as an architect. Burned in 1762, it was immediately rebuilt to Smibert's plan, and once again serves not only as a town hall but as a market, with the stalls of butchers, fishmongers, fruiterers, and greengrocers lining the lower floor.

A curious story attaches to the Faneuil Hall weathervane, a survivor of the fire. It seems that Sir Thomas Gresham, founder of the Royal Exchange in London, was abandoned as a baby and discovered in a field by children chasing grasshoppers. Taking the insect as an emblem of his salvation, he had a grasshopper weathervane set atop the Exchange. Peter Faneuil, later a member of the Exchange and an admirer of Gresham, liked the symbol and had a replica put up on Faneuil Hall. Or so the story goes.

Faneuil Hall's grasshopper weathervane.

"We next viewed the new Market House, an elegant building of brick, with a cupola on top ... This was built at the proper expense of one Faneuil, a substantial merchant of this place, lately dead, and presented by him to the public. It is called by the name of Faneuil Hall."

ALEXANDER HAMILTON, DIARIST (NOT THE STATESMAN), 1744

Where to Dine and Find Lodgings in Boston

As the most commonly visited place in New England, the city of Boston is amply supplied with taverns and inns. One venerable establishment, popular with travelers and townsmen alike since late in the last century, is The Bunch of Grapes, on the corner of King Street and Mackrell Lane. It is known as the "best punch house in Boston," and at present is run by Mrs. Rebecca Coffin. Her larder is amply stocked with fowls, puddings, mutton, and beef, and carving is done at the table – each guest serves himself from whatever part of the joint he prefers.

It was here at The Grapes that the first lodge of Freemasons in the city was organized, in 1733. A word of advice, however: this is a Whig tavern, where those with Tory sympathies might feel less than welcome.

THIRSTY FROM THE START

The first tavern in Boston was opened by Samuel Cole in 1634. It stood on Cornhill, near the corner of School Street. Later known as the Ship Tavern, it was the starting point of the great Boston fire of 1711.

Another favorite spot offering good food and drink, and comfortable lodging, is the Brackett family's Cromwell's Head, on School Street near King's Chapel. You won't be able to miss the place – its sign, which of course depicts the late Lord Protector, hangs so low before the entrance that you must either duck down low or risk toppling your hat and wig (a "wig" tavern, this) as you enter. We can assume the Cromwell's Head has commodious beds, because it was the lodging place of young Lieutenant Colonel George Washington, serving in the recent war with the French, when he came here a few years ago for a military conference with Governor Shirley. As Colonel Washington is said to be well over 6 feet in height, Mr. Brackett's bed must have answered the challenge.

The Green Dragon, on Union Street, hangs a fierce metal dragon from its impressive brick façade; and here Whig sentiments run similarly fierce, as likely as dragon's breath to scorch Parliament's breeches. If, however, your taste is more for a Tory place of refreshment, try the Royal Exchange, on the southwest corner of King and Exchange streets. A favorite retreat of British officers and smartly dressed young men of means, it's no place for seditious talk. And if its Masonic company you want, you can be sure of meeting brothers at Vardy's, just opposite the State House. There is something for everyone at Boston's taverns and inns.

HEADING NORTH FROM BOSTON

One of the most reliable of the post roads is the one that connects Boston with Portsmouth – your main route if you're heading from the Massachusetts capital to points north.

Regular stagecoach service along the Boston to Portsmouth route was established in 1761, when Mr. Bartholomew Stavers of the New Hampshire capital announced that for "the encouragement of trade from Portsmouth to Boston" he was providing "a large stage chair with two good horses well equipped." At present, the conveyance can carry up to six passengers. Mr. Stavers had a ready partner in his enterprise, as he is the brother of John Stavers, whose Earl of Halifax Inn, at Portsmouth, is the route's northern terminus.

The trip, costing some 13s. 6d., begins each Thursday morning on the Charlestown side of the ferry from Boston, and continues on to the pleasant outlying town of Medford. Some 6 miles north of Boston, Medford is a major junction point for stage routes leading not only along the coast to Portsmouth and on into Maine, but to other points in eastern New Hampshire and northeastern Massachusetts. It affords the comfortable stopping place of the Fountain Inn, a bustling and hospitable building nestled under great shade trees, with the odd and inviting innovation of elevated platforms and walkways linking their branches and connecting to the inn.

Bewitched No Longer

From Medford, the stage route continues along a good, hard-packed gravel road through Saugus, where the colonies' first iron foundry was built more than a century ago, and on through the farmlands of Lynn to Salem, 15 miles distant. Salem is still notorious for the witch trials held in the nineties of the last century, although the alleged offenses actually took place in Danvers

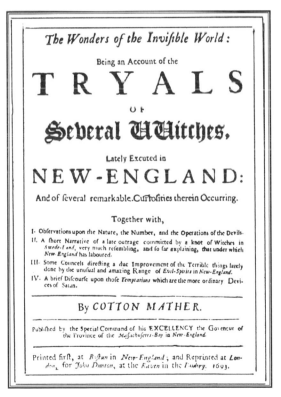

Rev. Cotton Mather described the Salem witch trials in this 1693 pamphlet.

Salem's busy waterfront, late in the colonial era.

village, somewhat to the west, then considered a part of Salem. But it is in Salem itself that you can still see old Judge Corwin's house, on Essex Street, home of the stern magistrate who sent the "witches" to their deaths.

In our more enlightened day, Salem is far more renowned for its merchant shipping, as we can readily gather from its town motto, "The wealth of the Indies to the uttermost gulf." If you plan to spend time in Salem (Mr. Stavers' coach will pick you up on its next weekly run), you can grasp some idea of the business of this lively port by strolling down to the central wharves, on Salem harbor, where ships calling from that "uttermost gulf" unload their ample cargoes. Facing the wharves is the lavish new home of one of the principals in this lucrative trade, Mr. Richard Derby. Built of brick, with its pedimented entrance and two pairs of chimneys, the mansion is situated so that Mr. Derby can keep a close eye on the comings and goings of his vessels – and those of his competitors.

A HOUSE WITH A LITERARY FUTURE

If you have time to tarry in Salem, walk east beyond the wharves for a look at one of the town's oldest houses, a dark forbidding structure that has stood for a century, and contrasts sharply with the elegant Derby mansion. You can't miss this old wooden pile – just look for a house with seven steep gables.

For lodging in Salem, try the Black Horse Tavern, a capacious inn warmed by a great central hearth; or Mrs. Abigail Brown's Tavern, known for its flip, punch, and a refreshing wine concoction called "sangrey."

An interesting side-trip from Salem takes you to Marblehead, situated on the rocky peninsula that protects Salem harbor from the open waters of Massachusetts Bay. Instead of great merchant vessels, Marblehead is the home of a fishing fleet, manned by hardy descendants of Cornishmen and emigrants from the Channel Islands. As a Marbleheader was once heard to exclaim, "Our ancestors came not here for religion. Their main end was to catch fish." Its fishy origins aside, the village boasts several impressive private homes: the opulent mansion

Marblehead's "King" Robert Hooper; portrait by Copley.

of "King" Robert Hooper, who got his name from his style of living, is by far the finest. After taking in the bracing sea air and views of Cape Ann from Marblehead Neck, you can stop for refreshment at the Fountain Inn, the very same tavern where Sir Harry Frankland first met his beautiful Agnes Surriage, an encounter we've described on page 42.

Continue on with the Stavers coach for another 15 miles, from Salem to Ipswich. Here is where Mr. Stavers puts his passengers up for the night, on their two-day journey from Boston to Portsmouth. At Ipswich, once a frontier village known as Agawam, your coach will pass over the substantial new stone bridge that spans the Ipswich River. Nearby is another brooding survivor of the earliest period of New England building, the Whipple House, said to date from 1640. Those were the days when a scant twelve adventurous emigrants settled this picturesque spot, at the threshold of a vast estuary where salt hay is harvested on tidal marshland. Despite its remoteness, the little community oddly thrived as a literary center in those early days. Nathaniel Ward wrote his pious *Simple Cobbler of Agawam* here, and it was the home of the remarkable poetess Anne Bradstreet, the "Tenth Muse Recently Sprung up in America," who amidst her "Meditations Divine and Moral" and other religious musings, still managed to write, in "To My Dear and Loving Husband,"

If ever two were one, then surely we.
If ever man were lov'd by wife, then thee ..."

Even in grim Puritan times, there was room for earthly ardor.

NAMES CARRIED OVER

The towns a British visitor might travel through on a trip to New England will have a very familiar ring: the naming of communities such as Ipswich, Plymouth, Yarmouth, Cambridge, and dozens of others shows that the settlers were more than a little nostalgic for home.

And what about Boston? It's a contraction of St. Botolph's Town – Botolph is the patron saint of Boston in Lincolnshire.

There are several inns at Ipswich, which is not remarkable given its position as a likely stopping place between Boston and Portsmouth. We're not certain which hostelry the Stavers enterprise favors at the moment, but the options include the Ross Tavern, on a busy street in the center of town, under the spreading branches of a great elm, that most characteristic of New England village trees; and Treadwell's Tavern, where, says John Adams, "Landlord and landlady are some of the grandest people alive." We're not sure, but we suspect young lawyer Adams is gently tweaking his host and hostess for their lofty airs – Mrs. Treadwell is, he points out, "the great-grand-daughter of Governor Endicott," and is evidently not above reminding her patrons of the fact.

And so up early, to skirt the salt marshes along the way to Newbury. Along this stretch of the route, during the haying season of summer and early autumn, you may see Essex County farm families and even people from as far as New Hampshire harvesting salt hay, prized as feed for their animals, and stacking it in great round stacks that dot the marshlands (the hay is hauled away by ox-drawn sleds when the marshes freeze in winter). Farther east across the marshes, meandering saltwater streams empty into Plum Island Sound. Beyond lies narrow Plum Island itself, wooded once with white pines that have long since been cut for ships' masts and lumber, and later used for grazing cattle. In our day it is a sandy waste, beaten along its far shore by the fierce Atlantic.

THE GREAT IPSWICH FRIGHT

During the next decade, in the opening days of the American Revolution, the road from Ipswich to Newbury and beyond became the scene of a great exercise in unfounded mob terror called the "Great Ipswich Fright." Here's how it happened: on April 20, 1775, just after the battles of Lexington and Concord, a rumor spread that British troops had landed on the coast north of Boston and were approaching Ipswich. The inhabitants fled in terror, rousing the villagers of Rowley, Newbury, Amesbury, and Salisbury as they headed north. So great was the commotion that in each successive town, residents thought the approaching hoard was the advancing enemy. But the alarm had turned out to be entirely false, and the tide of embarrassed householders receded back to their communities on the following day.

Having traveled 10 miles north of Ipswich your coach will cross the Parker River bridge into Newbury. It was just east of here, near where Newbury Old Town clusters around the Lower Green, that Reverend Thomas Parker and the town's first settlers landed in 1635. Over the next century, most of their descendants moved north to the area around the Upper Green. Watch for the stone milepost here that shows that you have completed more than half of your journey from Boston: on the side facing south is the carved inscription "P 30," meaning that Portsmouth is 30 miles distant; on the opposite side, the stone bears the legend "B 37."

Newbury, Massachusetts: 37 miles to Boston.

"Richard Thurlow, having built a bridge at his owne cost, over Newbury [Parker] River, hath liberty to take 2d. for every horse, cow, oxe ... that shall pass over said bridge ... provided that passengers shall be free."

EDICT OF THE MASSACHUSETTS GENERAL COURT, 1654, CONCERNING THE ORIGINAL BRIDGE OVER THE PARKER RIVER AT NEWBURY

A Bustling Port on the Merrimack

But most of the early Newbury families moved 2 miles farther north, to the mouth of the Merrimack River at Newburyport, which separated from its smaller parent community in 1764, and became a city in its own right. There they built prosperous shipyards, and went to sea as fishermen and whalers. The docks of Newburyport are today among New England's busiest, and over the course of the past century well over a hundred vessels have been launched here.

Newburyport is a lively, workaday place in the precincts near the harbor, but its neighborhoods grow quieter and more gracious along the streets ascending the hill leading away from the waterfront towards the High Street – the thoroughfare along which your coach will enter the community. It is a city of handsome churches, among them St. Paul's, at the corner of Market Street and the High Street, seat of one of the oldest Church of England parishes in New England. Of even greater interest is the Old South Church, built in the last decade at the corner of King and School streets in the city's south end. One of the founders of Old South was the great British evangelist, Reverend George Whitefield, who first arrived in Newburyport in 1740 and preaches here whenever he is in the vicinity. The church has an exceptionally fine three-tiered steeple.

If your driver stops in Newburyport for refreshment, his favorite retreat will likely be the Wolfe Tavern, at the corner of Fish Street and Threadneedle Alley. This fine establishment, opened in 1762, was named by its landlord William Davenport after General James Wolfe, who so sadly lost his life in the successful British assault on Quebec that turned the tide of our war against the French for control of Canada (see Plate v). Mr. Davenport,

Newburyport's Old South Church, renowned for its handsome steeple.

in fact, was captain of a colonial militia company that fought under Wolfe's command. You can't miss the place – at its doorway hangs a massive signboard, bearing the general's likeness, carved by the proprietor himself.

Well regarded for its rum punch (made with rum from Newburyport's own distilleries), egg toddies, and good wine, the Wolfe Tavern serves up brisk conversation along with its hearty dinners. This is where all Newburyport gathers to thrash out the issues of the day, and where everyone from the Freemasons to the Marine Society holds their regular meetings.

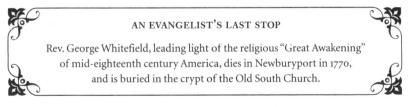

AN EVANGELIST'S LAST STOP

Rev. George Whitefield, leading light of the religious "Great Awakening" of mid-eighteenth century America, dies in Newburyport in 1770, and is buried in the crypt of the Old South Church.

Leaving Newburyport, you'll cross the Merrimack River near its mouth by means of a sailing ferry, arriving in the small village of Salisbury. This is the last of the Massachusetts towns along this route, and marks the beginning of a flat, barren country that meets the sea, a scant 3 miles to the east, along an apron of marshland threaded through by sluggish tidal streams.

CALLING THE FERRYMAN

Not all ferrying is conducted under sail. Ferries attached by rope to either shore are in use wherever crossing distances are fairly short, and river currents are swift. Where traffic is heavy, two boats are often in service, one on each bank. You can call the ferryman by hollering "Haloo," by ringing a bell, or even by building a fire on the bank. His rates are fixed by the colony's general assembly, so it's a good idea to know just what you should be paying ahead of time.

The only settlement of any size between Salisbury and Portsmouth, some 19 miles distant, is Hampton Falls, a community renowned for its bustling sawmills, shingle mills, and gristmills. It's also an important post town, where stagecoaches – yours included – stop for a change of horses before continuing on their way to Portsmouth or Boston. It's likely your driver will make the change at Wells Tavern, where forty coach horses are stabled. Horses, in fact, have long been an important part of life at Hampton Falls: the first horse show in New Hampshire was held here in 1726.

Hampton, 4 miles further north, is one of New Hampshire's four original towns, and in its early days was sorely vexed by Indian attacks. Breakfast Hill, in North Hampton, is so named because of a reversal of the Indians' fortunes, on a morning in 1696 when one of their raiding parties was surprised by militiamen while they were eating breakfast. The Indians were killed, and their captives were rescued. As your coach clatters north toward Portsmouth, you'll undoubtedly find it hard to imagine that such desperate battles raged upon this now peaceful landscape, within the lifetimes of people still living today.

The Aristocratic Charms of Portsmouth

The Post Road enters Portsmouth through its "back door," on the inland side, but no traveler will take long to discover that this is a city where the sea and seaborne commerce are all-important. Some twenty-five vessels are launched in Portsmouth each year, and many more arrive and depart with the cargoes – including the great naval masts from the interior forests – that have made the city wealthy. It's also the capital of New Hampshire, which since 1741 has had its own governor and has been entirely independent of Massachusetts.

Portsmouth, New Hampshire's capital, seen from across the Piscataqua.

The Earl of Halifax Inn, terminus of the stage route from Boston, stands at the corner of Court and Atkinson streets near the waterfront. Take a moment to enjoy Mr. John Stavers' hospitality and ale – and to arrange your lodgings – and then walk the short way to Market Square, the real center of the city, where any tour of Portsmouth is best begun. Here is the State House, where the provincial assembly meets; and here is where that perhaps equally important assembly – of citizens meeting, greeting, shopping, and exchanging the news of the day – is always in session. From Market Square it's only a short walk to Bow Street and Ceres Street, which front the busy harbor; and here, where the mouth of the Piscataqua River opens onto the oceans of the world, it's easy to spend half a day or more watching the big ships load and unload their cargoes.

It was for just that purpose that Captain John Moffat recently built the grand mansion opposite the docks on Market Street, behind Ceres, as a wedding present for his son Samuel. Samuel Moffatt, a shipowner and importer of British goods, enjoys sitting with his business colleagues by the big windows in the second-floor parlor of his opulent home, keeping a sharp eye on the wharves. If you can possibly obtain an invitation to the Moffat home, you'll marvel at the remarkable craftsmanship that went into its every detail – intricate woodcarving, richly detailed ornamental plasterwork, imported French wallpapers, and a magnificent paneled staircase, all of a piece with what John

Adams, with his Quincy Puritan's gimlet eye for worldly splendor, called "the pomps and vanities of that little world, Portsmouth."

MOFFAT DUCKS OUT

Samuel Moffat didn't enjoy his new house for long. Overburdened with debt in 1768, he fled to the West Indies to avoid his creditors. His father reclaimed the mansion, and lived there until his death at the age of 94.

We also recommend that you call upon whatever connections you may have to secure invitations to the home of the Honorable Jonathan Warner, an imposing brick edifice at the corner of Chapel and Daniel streets notable for its murals depicting scenes as diverse as Governor Phipps on horseback, a pair of Mohawk Indians, and Abraham about to sacrifice Isaac; and to the new water-front home of Thomas Wentworth, a wedding present from his mother (these Portsmouth grandees seem fond of lavishing houses on their offspring when they marry). Three master carvers labored for more than a year on the interior woodwork, the wallpapers are hand-painted, and there are no fewer than eleven fireplaces, many bordered in Delft tiles. The splendid linden tree that graces the front lawn was brought from England by a ship that docked almost at the mansion's door. Such are the perquisites of a Portsmouth shipowner.

You will have to travel south of the city proper, to a point of land that juts into the outer harbor, if you have an opportunity to visit the most famous Portsmouth residence of all, that of Governor Benning Wentworth (see page 24). The governor loves his rambling, forty-room seaside home, and even uses one of his parlors for meetings of his council – we can only imagine how scandalized the stern pioneers of a century ago would have been, at the thought of

the councilors being distracted by the sculpted ladies, in high buxom relief, that flank the fireplace. The greatest distraction in the high-living governor's residence, though, is probably his ample punch-bowl, always filled for drinking the King's health. And outdoors, his prettiest indulgence is his lilac bushes, the first imported from England.

Council Chamber hearth, Governor Wentworth's mansion.

John Singleton Copley's 1767 painting of Nicholas Boylston is perhaps the best portrayal of a Boston merchant prince taking his ease. Boylston's silk finery is available only to the wealthiest New Englanders.

Anne Fairchild Bowler, another of Copley's well-to-do clients, resides on a country estate in Portsmouth, Rhode Island, with her husband, Metcalf Bowler.

James Peake's *1761 engraving,* Beginning of an American Settlement or Farm, *depicts a scene repeated countless times as New England's wilderness gave way to civilization.*

John Smibert's View of Boston, *1738. The Scottish-born Smibert's talents also extended to architecture; he was the designer of Boston's Faneuil Hall. Smibert died in 1751, and is interred in the city's Old Granary Burial Ground.*

Major General James Wolfe, the British commander killed during the 1759 battle for Quebec, has been a popular namesake for taverns throughout New England. This sign graced an establishment in Brooklyn, Connecticut.

Tavern signs need appeal to the illiterate as well as those who can read, as recognized by Mr. A. Bissell, proprietor of the Bull's Head in East Windsor, Connecticut.

Is he wondering how much to charge – or pondering the political issues that engross him as much as his silversmithing? One of John Singleton Copley's most famous portraits is this frank study of Paul Revere.

John Townsend of Newport, Rhode Island, is one of New England's foremost cabinetmakers. This exquisite kneehole desk displays his signature "block and shell" style.

*"The place of my residence is within a mile of … the harbor …
and no vessel can come into port without coming into my sight, which
… has contributed in great measure to the chastity of the port."*

GOVERNOR BENNING WENTWORTH

The Inland Wilds of New Hampshire

The interior spaces of New Hampshire are slowly being populated, although the farther you travel from the coast, the fewer settlers you will encounter in the rough new towns. Don't expect any public conveyance to take you very far into New Hampshire's wilds, as the communities are connected by trails best negotiated on horseback or on foot. Far to the north, the White Mountains are all but impenetrable, and the few inhabitants are true pioneers. Their home is with the moose and the bear, the catamount and lynx.

INTO THE WILDS

Access to New Hampshire's interior was to be greatly improved by Governor John Wentworth, Benning's nephew and successor, who will build a 45-mile road from Portsmouth to his summer residence on Lake Wentworth in the late 1760s. In 1771, the Governor will extend the road to Hanover, on the Connecticut River, so that he could attend the first commencement exercises at Dartmouth College.

The White Mountains will not prove to be entirely impenetrable, as they are cut through north to south by three great notches. In 1771, a moose hunter named Timothy Nash will discover one of the notches, later named after the pioneer Crawford family, and report his find to Governor Wentworth. The Governor will make an agreement with Nash to give him a tract of land if he can bring a horse through his notch and all the way to Portsmouth, a feat which Nash will accomplish by using a rope sling to lower the animal over the steepest mountain ledges.

On into Maine

If your plans call for a further excursion into the vast territory of Maine, you will likely begin by crossing the broad mouth of the Piscataqua River by ferry, arriving at Kittery. The road extends all the way north to the remote coastal outpost of Machias, although the farther north you travel, the rougher the road becomes. Since 1757, there has been a postal route over the 50 miles between Portsmouth and Falmouth, Maine, but stagecoach service is infrequent along this route. (After all, there are scarcely 25,000 people in all of Maine, and it was only in 1760 that a treaty was finally signed with the last hostile Indians.) Many travelers opt instead for the water route, taking passage on a ship bound "down east" for points along the rugged Maine coast. No wonder: even if you have a decent mount, you will likely agree with Circuit Judge John Adams, who describes the coastal road as consisting of "many sharp, steep hills, many rocks, many deep ruts," and his trip as "vastly disagreeable."

SAILING "DOWN EAST"

Sailors following a northeast course along the Maine coast speak of heading "down east." Why "down"? It's because of the prevailing winds, which blow from the southwest and carry them "down" the coast. It won't be long before that entire deeply indented, rocky shoreline – and even the future state of Maine itself – bears the nickname "Down East."

Lt. Gen. Sir Wm. Pepperell, Bart. The Victor of Louisbourg A.D. 1745.

Kittery, like Portsmouth, is a shipbuilding town, British warships being one of its specialties. It's defended by the formidable Fort William, which looms above a granite promontory at Kittery Point. It was named for Sir William Pepperell, a hero of Louisbourg and prominent local official whose widow, Lady Pepperell, has recently built a mansion in the best classical style on Pepperell Road overlooking Portsmouth harbor.

William Pepperell, shown here in a portrait by Smibert, was the first native-born American baronet.

A GREAT NAVAL LEGACY

Kittery continued in the business of building naval vessels long after the days of wooden ships was over. Since 1800, it has been the home of the Portsmouth Naval Shipyard, which launched ships for the U.S. Navy until the 1960s, and remains important as a repair and maintenance facility.

Maine's Prospering Port

Aside from possible stops at small but charming communities such as York, Wells (Jefferds' Tavern is recommended) and Kennebunkport, your vessel's principal port of call along the Maine coast will be Falmouth, which stands at the head of Casco Bay. If you have come north by land, you'll find a ferry at Cape Elizabeth that will allow you to complete the trip to Falmouth.

Falmouth is a great exporter of fish, furs, and lumber, especially mast trees for naval and merchant vessels alike. The largest of these masts, 100 feet or more in height, lately fetch prices in excess of £200. To get an idea of just how lucrative the mast business can be, walk down Westbrook Street on Falmouth Neck to see George Tate's fine new mansion. Mr. Tate's business? He is the mast agent for the Royal Navy.

West Indian sugar mills produced molasses, the basis for New England rum.

The port also receives volumes of West Indies molasses, which its distilleries turn into potent rum. Codfish, salted and dried, is shipped to the Caribbean in return. All of this merchandise – freshly hewn lumber, sweet molasses, curing fish – lends a distinctive aroma to the salt air of Falmouth Neck. If this atmosphere appeals to you – and if you have time to tarry, perhaps amusing yourself by watching masts being loaded through the stern ports of the special ships that carry them and observing all the other business of this lively harbor – you can find lodging at the establishment of Moses Pearson, a prosperous wharf owner who also serves as sheriff of Cumberland County. That title, we assume, will assure the traveler that his is not a disorderly house.

SOMEDAY, MAINE'S LARGEST CITY

After the American Revolution – during which Falmouth was burned by the British – the part of the town called Falmouth Neck was incorporated as Portland.

Beyond Falmouth, the Maine seaboard grows ever wilder and more deeply indented – if all of the ins and outs of its bays and peninsulas were to be straightened, the coastline would likely reach to Europe and beyond. Castine and Machias lie farther "down east," and farther still, across the Gulf of Maine, stands the fledgling naval bastion of Halifax, in the British colony of Nova Scotia. In this direction, at least, your New England rambles – by land or sea – are at an end, unless you care to follow one of the territory's great rivers into the forbidding forests of the interior, where Indian pathways lead all the way to Quebec.

FROM BOSTON TO RHODE ISLAND AND CONNECTICUT

If you plan to head south, toward New Haven and perhaps all the way to New York (two days more of travel along the Post Road past New Haven), you have several choices of overland routes. One road leads to Providence, Rhode Island, at the head of Narragansett Bay, then south to New London and on along the Connecticut coast. Or, you could head south to Newport from Providence, and then west – but that route puts you in the hands of three different ferrymen. There are also inland routes. If you follow the Old Bay Road from

Boston to Springfield, you can travel south from there to New Haven by way of Hartford and Meriden. Connecticut people on their way to or from Boston often prefer the road that cuts through the colony's northeastern corner – but there you'll be taking your chances with the dangerous crossings of the Quinebaug and Shetucket rivers, which run especially wild in springtime.

~~~

"The time may come when the public will support a stage between Hartford and Boston, but not in your day or mine."

REMARK MADE TO LEVI SOMERS, A PROPONENT OF
REGULAR STAGECOACH SERVICE BETWEEN HARTFORD,
BOSTON, AND NEW HAVEN, IN AROUND 1783

~~~

The Way to Providence and Newport

The two cities of Boston and Providence, being scarce more than 50 miles apart, have benefited from a stagecoach service for many years. The route is not difficult, extending as it does through a fairly level country of pine woods and farmland, and the journey may be made in a single day.

Leaving before sunrise, and heading out of Boston on the Post Road by way of the suburban village of Roxbury, the stage reaches Dedham, 11 miles from Boston, where the lower, middle, and upper roads part ways. Dedham is where Dr. Nathaniel Ames, the renowned author of almanacs, keeps a comfortable tavern at the Sign of the Sun, and this is where you might take a quick breakfast. Horses will likely be changed at Walpole, another 10 miles distant and near the halfway point between the Massachusetts capital and your destination.

Attleboro is the last Massachusetts town along the Post Road before it enters the colony of Rhode Island. Had you come this way a century and a quarter ago, you would have seen stark evidence of how seriously differences of religion were taken in that less sophisticated age. Here stood a marker that proclaimed, "Beyond this line Roger Williams may not go." Williams, you may remember, was the unorthodox minister who had left the Massachusetts Bay colony over a doctrinal dispute, and established his Providence Plantations as a haven of religious freedom. Had he ventured north of here, things might have fared badly for him: those were the days when individuals deemed heretical in their opinions might find themselves swinging, like the Quaker

Mary Dyer, from that great oak on Boston Common. Today, of course, coaches pass unhindered between the two colonies, regardless of their passengers' doctrinal opinions. (A Quebec Jesuit heading into Massachusetts might press the point, however.)

A HERMIT REAPPEARS

Attleboro's earliest English settler was the reclusive Reverend William Blaxton, who had abandoned the future site of Boston when he felt it had become overcrowded by the arrival of Governor Winthrop's party in 1630. He eventually moved farther south, to Rhode Island.

A Visit to Providence

Providence stands at the point where its namesake river flows into the head of Narragansett Bay, that great irregular arm of the sea that renders the Rhode Island colony so fit for maritime commerce. Long gone are the days when "Providence Plantations" was a fit name for the settlement, as the city now turns its face not to its inland farms but to its busy wharves. The source of its prosperity – as with that of its great rival, Newport, at the other end of the bay – is the trade with Africa and the West Indies in molasses, rum, and slaves.

"It was not price nor money that could have purchased Rhode Island. Rhode Island was purchased by love."

ROGER WILLIAMS, FOUNDER OF THE COLONY OF RHODE ISLAND

The most vivid evidence of Providence's wealth and prominence may be found along Benefit Street, laid out scarcely a decade ago but already ornamented with the fine homes of the city's most prominent merchants and shipowners. The street runs just east of Towne Street, the city's main thoroughfare; both streets follow the course of the Providence River as it flows over its final mile to the harbor.

The most important edifice on Benefit Street is the new State House, just finished in 1762. It stands between Benefit and Towne streets, at Court Street, and replaced the Old Colony House after that venerable structure's destruction by fire in 1758. Solidly built of brick and brownstone with painted wood trim, the State House might strike some visitors as somewhat behind the

Newport's Colony House, where Rhode Island's governor usually presides.

times in terms of style, owing more to the taste of Queen Anne's time than the present. But we're not in London, and fashion does lag a bit when it crosses the Atlantic.

A more important concern might be: why build a seat for the colony's General Assembly in Providence, when the capital is at Newport? The answer is that Rhode Island doesn't have just one capital. Newport, the grander of the colony's two major centers of population, erected a "Colony House" as early as 1690, and it's where you're most likely to find the governor today. But Rhode Island's legislators actually meet in rotation at various places around the small colony, no doubt so as not to arouse any jealousy among its communities. The citizens of Massachusetts, which is far larger and more populous, must find this an amusingly extreme extent to take democracy – as far as we know, no one in Newburyport, Salem, or Gloucester is envious of Boston's claim on the Great and General Court.

THE CAPITAL COULDN'T SIT STILL

Rhode Island would remain scrupulously devoted to its idea of a roving legislature even in the years after statehood. Up until 1854, meetings of the Assembly were to rotate between Newport, South Kingstown, Bristol, East Greenwich, and Providence. Newport and Providence would be co-capitals until 1900, after which the sole honor finally went to Providence.

Roger Williams founded his settlement near a freshwater spring at the point where the Woonasquatucket and Moshassuck rivers meet to form the Providence. But today Market Square, tucked between Towne Street and the river a few blocks south of Williams' spring, is the commercial heart of Providence. This is where farmers from the surrounding countryside bring their produce to sell, and where the news of the city and the colony circulates on market days. Facing the Square is the spacious home of Mr. Jabez Bowen, prominent in civic affairs and an accomplished amateur astronomer, who is said to be planning to set up a telescope at Providence with which to observe the transit of the planet Venus across the sun in 1769. On a more terrestrial note, it was from Mr. Bowen's balcony that the accession of King George III to the throne was announced in 1760.

Copley's portrait of Jabez Bowen, a leading citizen of Newport.

For lodging and refreshment at Providence, two establishments can be recommended. Mowry's Tavern has stood atop a hill on Abbott Street, just north of the city proper, since the time of King Philip's War a century ago. Since then, many a traveler has been warmed at the tavern's great stone hearth, whose tall chimney is a local landmark. Closer to Market Square and the waterfront stands the Sabin Tavern, on Towne Street.

CELESTIAL CITY

Jabez Bowen and two other Providence astronomers did observe the 1769 transit of Venus. Two Providence streets, Planet and Transit, were named in honor of the event.

On to Newport

If you wish to continue south from Providence to Newport, you are advised to make your way by water. Narragansett Bay is crisscrossed by any number of packets on a regular sailing schedule, and the voyage south to the city at the mouth of the bay is easier and more pleasant than the overland route along the eastern shore, which in any event would involve ferry passage from the mainland to Aquidneck Island – the actual "Rhode" Island, named after its counterpart in the Aegean.

Newport enjoys as grand a seaside location as any city in New England, and its harbor is well protected from the open waters of Long Island Sound by the fishhook shape of its peninsula. It has prospered consistently from its founding in 1639, building its trade first on wool, fish, and the products of Aquidneck Island farms, and more recently on the slave trade, in which Rhode Island is more active than any of the other New England colonies. Here also are distilleries producing rum, and works for making candles from the sperm whale oil that Newport's captains deliver to her wharves.

Newport possesses a remarkably mixed population – along with the English settlers who were first to arrive, it has added to its numbers Jews from the Dutch colonies in the Caribbean (see page 114), free blacks, and, lately, a great many Scottish immigrants. Adding to its cosmopolitan character is a summer community of plantation owners from the American South, who repair here to escape the oppressive climate of their home colonies.

One of the first things you will notice, when you step off your packet and head into town, are the paving stones that banish mud from Newport's streets. The principal avenues have been paved for a half century, a sure sign that this is a place long accustomed to prosperity.

WHERE THE MONEY WAS

The paving of Newport's streets was financed by a tax on the slave trade. Of all the New England colonies, Rhode Island prospers the most from the traffic in African slaves.

If you require any further evidence of the city's worldly success, stroll up Long Wharf past Thames Street to Colony House, the seat of the General Assembly when it meets in Newport. When it was built, a quarter-century ago, masonry edifices were quite rare in Rhode Island – and this one boasts not only bricks, but bricks imported from England. Trimmed in sandstone, its pedimented balcony ornamented with a gilded pineapple and its paneled chambers adorned with fine woodcarving, Colony House seems to throw down the challenge to Rhode Island's humbler seats of government, as if Newport and Newport alone should hold the honor of capital. And nearly all Newporters you will meet would be inclined to agree.

Trinity Church, like Colony House designed by the accomplished Richard Munday, stands as the foremost home of the Church of England in a city and colony famous for tolerance of diverse denominations. Its magnificent steeple, surmounted with a golden crown, contains the very first church bell to have rung in New England. The bell was a gift of Queen Anne in 1709, and was installed in the present structure in 1725.

God and the civil government aren't the only beneficiaries of Newport's indulgence in fine building. Some years ago, Mr. Abraham Redwood financed the purchase of books for the city's philosophical society. This was the beginning of the Redwood Library, a home for which was built in 1750 on Bellevue Avenue between Church and Mill streets. A curious new style was adopted for the library by its architect, Mr. Peter Harrison (who also designed Newport's Touro Synagogue). It resembles nothing so much as a Greek temple, with a simple triangular portico raised upon four Doric columns. But this is, after all, a temple of learning, so the classical influence does seem appropriate.

Newport's Redwood Library, housing Abraham Redwood's bequest of books.

The prolific Mr. Harrison also designed what is perhaps Newport's grandest private dwelling, the new home of Deputy Governor Jonathan Nichols, facing the waterfront at the foot of Poplar Street. This exquisite mansion – above its doorway is another carved pineapple, that favorite symbol of hospitality in Newport and throughout New England – boasts a magnificent three-story staircase, a marble fireplace, and furnishings crafted of the finest mahogany by John Townsend and John Goddard, master cabinetmakers at Easton's Point near here.

Newport's pre-eminent tavern, and its oldest, is the White Horse, at the corner of Farewell and Marlborough streets. Founded nearly a century ago by one William Mayes, it was later owned by his son, William Jr., who had previously earned his living by piracy. The White Horse under subsequent owners has long since settled into respectability, and assures its patrons good board, excellent drink, and comfortable lodgings.

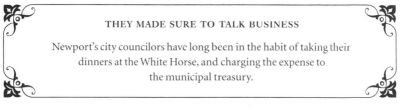

THEY MADE SURE TO TALK BUSINESS

Newport's city councilors have long been in the habit of taking their dinners at the White Horse, and charging the expense to the municipal treasury.

At the White Horse or elsewhere, one potion you're sure to encounter in a Newport tavern is the city's own favorite concoction, Newport Punch. Every landlord has his own variation, but the essential ingredients never vary – rum, lime juice, arrack, and sugar. A great refreshment in summer, it's kept cool by storage in stone vessels immersed in tavern wells.

Routes to Connecticut

If you are not returning to Providence before continuing your journey into Connecticut, your option will be to leave Newport by ferry, proceeding west first to Conanicut Island, and then, having crossed the small island with its village of Jamestown, taking ferry passage again to the mainland at Kingston. This is an arduous route, which will leave you still more than 40 miles short of the nearest substantial Connecticut town of New London, in a corner of New England not favored with regular coach service – and, we should add, the Thames River is the last obstacle that must be ferried before New London is finally reached.

Far more to be recommended is the overland route from Providence to New London, covering some 60 miles. The road extends from Providence across the farms and forests of the little colony by way of Scituate and Coventry. Depending on the weather and your conveyance, the trip might be made in one day or two; but should you need to spend the night at a tavern in Scituate called the Black Horse, be advised that one of the upstairs chambers is said to be haunted by the ghost of an Indian, who has been known to pull sleeping guests by the hair and frighten them with his tomahawk. So far as we know, none of the patrons of the Black Horse has actually been scalped, which is more than can be said for those unfortunates who stop for room and board at Scituate's other inn, the Pine Tree. The Pine Tree, we are told, sets a dreadful table. Indian ghosts aside, the food at the Black Horse is reputed to be excellent.

Down the Thames to New London

The first town of substance on the Connecticut side of the colonial border is Norwich, 17 miles upstream from Long Island Sound on the Thames River. Despite its inland situation, Norwich still lies on the navigable portion of the Thames, and has had success at shipbuilding and whaling; but its easy access from the sea has recently brought it a more unusual distinction. Some ten years ago, after Britain had expelled the French settlers from their "Acadia" in Nova Scotia, many of the Acadians came south to swell the population of Norwich. Perhaps even stranger was the more recent migration of English Norwalk families in the opposite direction – to Nova Scotia, where they have founded several new towns. The reason for this exodus is the already diminished supply of good farmland in this part of Connecticut, a fact which the displaced Acadians were not at liberty to take into consideration.

If you have the opportunity, travel the 10 miles from Norwich to Lebanon, which lies to the northwest. Here is the seat of the Trumbull family, whose gracious home speaks well of their success in Caribbean trade; and also Mr. Nathan Tisdale's Academy, an institution of such excellence that it has attracted students from as far as the West Indies. Lebanon is also remarkable for its 100-acre town common, which stretches a mile in length.

Continuing south along the Thames we reach New London, built around a fine deep harbor at the river's mouth. As might be surmised from its location, this is a town of sailors and shipbuilders, and merchants venturing in foreign trade. The first printing press in Connecticut was set up here in 1709, and today the town's Mr. Timothy Green does a brisk business in almanacs, and in publishing Mr. Roger Sherman's "Astronomical Diary."

"About seven that evening, we come to New London Ferry: here, by reason of a very high wind, we met with great difficulty in getting over – the boat tos't exceedingly, and our horses caper'd at a very surprising rate, and set us all in a fright."

SARAH KEMBLE KNIGHT,
JOURNAL OF A JOURNEY FROM BOSTON TO NEW YORK, 1704

New London was founded by John Winthrop, Jr., son of the illustrious Winthrop who was instrumental in the settlement of Boston; but young Winthrop's worldly ambitions for his new settlement seem to have exceeded his father's plans for a figurative "city on a hill." It was Winthrop Jr. who devised the name "New London," and who took the Pequot Monhegin River and christened it the Thames. But thus far – despite its crowded wharves, impressive grist mill, and the dignified homes of its prosperous merchants – it has not progressed nearly as far as the elder Winthrop's settlement, let alone its counterpart on that other Thames.

THEY TALK FUNNY OVER HERE/THERE

For evidence that Yankee speech is beginning to diverge from the English language as spoken in its homeland, consider the local pronunciation of "Thames." In Connecticut, the British "Tems" has been altered, with a full "Th" and a hard "a" to follow. One day, we suspect, Americans may speak an oddly different version of the mother tongue.

Leaving New London and heading west along Long Island Sound, it is possible to press onward toward New Haven and New York, with the necessary ferry crossing of the mouth of the Connecticut River at Lyme. But for now, let's return to Boston, and follow a route west and south that takes us through the heart of Massachusetts, and on to Connecticut's capital of Hartford.

THE POST ROAD FROM BOSTON TO SPRINGFIELD

The Post Road from Boston to Springfield begins by following the Charles River, and continues through the farms and village centers of Watertown and Waltham on its way to Sudbury, 25 miles distant from the capital. Travelers along this route know Sudbury as the place where Colonel Ezekiel Howe's establishment, the Red Horse Tavern, has been a reliable stop for food and lodging ever since 1686, when it was built by the colonel's ancestor, Samuel Howe. (*His* forebear, John Howe, was one of the original settlers of Sudbury who arrived from England on the *Confidence* in 1638.)

"The stage left Boston about three o'clock in the morning,
reaching the Sudbury Tavern for breakfast, a considerable portion
of the route being traveled in total darkness, and without your having
the least idea who your companion might be."
HENRY WADSWORTH LONGFELLOW, DESCRIBING THE 1840 COACH
TRIP ON WHICH HE FIRST VISITED THE FORMER RED HORSE TAVERN,
CHRONICLED IN HIS COLLECTION OF NARRATIVE POEMS
TITLED *TALES OF A WAYSIDE INN*

SIDE TRIP: TWO OUTLYING TOWNS

Although they aren't on the direct route from Boston to Springfield, there are two towns in the hinterlands west of Boston worth an overnight visit. These are Lexington and Concord, Middlesex County villages nestled amid gently rolling, well-tended farmland.

On the way to Lexington, you will likely wish to stop at Cambridge and the academic precincts of Harvard College some 13 miles west of Boston (see pages 115–17). In addition to "Harvard Yard" and its trim surrounding structures, Cambridge attractions include the spacious nearby Common, presided over by the stately new Christ Church (again, the work of architect Peter Harrison); and the splendid homes along the aristocratic Brattle Street. Major John Vassall's house (later the home of poet Henry Wadsworth Longfellow), with gardens reaching back to the Charles River, is perhaps the finest of the lot.

Major John Vassall's handsome new mansion, on Brattle Street in Cambridge.

Lexington, a bit more than 7 miles distant from Cambridge, clusters around an expansive village green, large enough for militia drills. As you will have traveled several hours, it's good to know that the town is well supplied with taverns; especially recommended are the century-old Buckman, directly on the Green; and the Munroe, somewhat less than a mile to the east.

Concord lies 7 miles farther west. Snugly circling its green like Lexington, it nevertheless best repays the visitor who cares to ride or ramble to its bucolic outer reaches, particularly the countryside to the north surrounding the Concord River. The rough wooden North Bridge affords a pleasant vantage point. An equally charming spot, south of town, is Walden Pond, its wooded shores perfect for moments of quiet contemplation. And fortunately, as a day trip from Boston would be impossible, Wright's Tavern in the village center provides overnight lodging and copious food and drink.

Colonel Howe's Red Horse is only one of several busy inns in Sudbury – the town is frequented by teamsters carrying Connecticut valley produce to the markets of Boston, as well as by mail-coaches such as yours – but it is easily the most popular. A vast taproom fills the ground floor, where a wooden portcullis rises and lowers incessantly over the bar, as tankards full and empty pass back and forth between landlord and patrons. Above are the chambers for travelers, and on a third story are garret quarters for slaves accompanying their masters, as well as a dance hall. Seldom are the servers and stable-boys of the Red Horse idle, as there is rarely a lull in traffic on the Post Road – but arrive at breakfast or dinner time, and the place is at its merriest and most fragrant with victuals fresh from oven and hearth.

"What do you think
Here is good drink,
Perhaps you may not know it,
If not in haste do stop and taste,
You merry folks will show it."

INSCRIPTION IN A WINDOW SASH AT THE RED HORSE TAVERN,
MADE BY PATRON WILLIAM MOLINEAUX JR. ON JUNE 24, 1774

The Post Road continues west by way of Marlborough, Westborough, and Shrewsbury, passing, at the latter, the impressive mansion of Artemas Ward, lately an officer in the war against the French and Indians. You are traveling through hillier regions than you have been accustomed to along the New England coast, and this more rugged terrain, along with the denser interior forests and many lakes and streams, will give you a better idea of the place as it was when encountered by the first English settlers, and help you understand why so many colonial villages still seem so isolated from each other. And you are traveling the Post Road – just imagine the seclusion of the farms and hamlets that lie along the less frequented roads and trails. It's no wonder that the families who live in these isolated communities, or coax crops from these rock-strewn acres, look forward so eagerly to their militia drills and election day celebrations, which we'll take a closer look at later in this guide (see Chapter 9).

INVITE YOUR FRIENDS

On a bitter chill day along the Post Road between Boston and Worcester, nothing is so rewarding as a stop at Brigham's Tavern in Westborough for a sampling of Mr. Brigham's famous hot mulled wine. If you'd like to make it at home, here is the recipe – although it will never taste as good as it does when you've just alighted from an ice-cold coach.

One quart of boiling hot Madeira
Half a pint of boiling water
Six eggs, beaten to a froth
Sugar to sweeten to taste
Gratings of nutmeg to flavor

From Worcester to Springfield

Having skirted the northern reaches of pretty Lake Quinsigamond (not all Indian names have been abandoned in favor of the English; this one means "fishing place for pickerel" in the Nipmuc tongue), you will soon arrive at Worcester, a long day's ride of 42 miles from Boston. Worcester, the principal town of central Massachusetts, has a remarkably long history for a place so far removed from the coast. Though its earliest English inhabitants were bedeviled by Indians in league with the French, their abandoned settlement was reclaimed by 1713, and has since grown to become the shire town of Worcester County. John Adams, the promising Boston lawyer whom we have quoted elsewhere in this guide, taught school here not long after his graduation from Harvard College.

THOMAS' TRIUMPHANT DAY

In July 1776, Worcester will be the first Massachusetts town in which the Declaration of Independence is publicly read. The reader will be Isaiah Thomas, publisher of the pro-independence *Massachusetts Spy* and later founder of the American Antiquarian Society.

Worcester is far enough to have traveled from Boston before nightfall, and we advise an evening's sojourn here – perhaps at Heywood's Tavern, on Salem Street, or at Thomas Stearns' King's Arms Tavern, which stands between Elm and Maple streets near the town center.

The next day's travel, covering 50 miles, will bring you to the town of Springfield, on the broad Connecticut River. Like the Atlantic coast, this great waterway has been a magnet for settlement; as you will no doubt have noticed while clattering over New England's rough roads, travel along the bays and rivers of these colonies is an altogether more practicable affair, especially when quantities of goods are involved. The country between Worcester and Springfield is still but sparsely settled, although you will pass through villages such as Auburn, Sturbridge, Palmer, and Wilbraham; and the reason is clearly its distance from both the coast and the Connecticut. Springfield itself communicates far more easily with Hartford and New Haven, south by way of the river and Long Island Sound, than with its own colonial capital of Boston.

English settlers reached Springfield remarkably early; William Pynchon and his band of twelve Puritan families arrived here in 1636, only six years after the founding of Boston. (In 1650, though, Pynchon returned to England after questions of theological error arose concerning a book he wrote.) The fragile outpost was burnt to the ground by the Indians during King Philip's War, with its destruction personally supervised by Philip himself from a stockade overlooking the river.

Springfield came back to life in the early eighteenth century and found its place as a river port and a mill town, sawing timber and grinding grain, and has lately prospered by making bricks from local deposits of clay. If any Massachusetts town has a future in manufacturing, residents believe, that town surely is Springfield. Some think that the production of firearms might be profitable. But others cannot imagine, now that the French and Indians have been routed, what the need would be for muskets in any great volume.

North and West from Springfield

Springfield is a good place for the traveler to pause and decide which way his ramblings might take him next. The way to civilization is the way south to Hartford and New Haven, which we will describe farther on in this guide. But for the truly adventurous, the promising horizons are to the west, and, especially, to the north. Our suggestion is to tarry for an evening or two, if you have the time, perhaps at Parson's Tavern on Court Street near the river. There, you might meet travelers experienced in the routes that lead to New England's frontiers.

❦

"Gen. Shepherd, Mr. Lyman and many other Gentlemen sat
an hour or two with me in the evening at Parson's Tavern,
where I lodged, and which is a good House."

FROM A DIARY ENTRY BY GEORGE WASHINGTON, DESCRIBING
A VISIT TO SPRINGFIELD IN 1774. AS PRESIDENT, WASHINGTON WOULD
SELECT THE SITE OF THE SPRINGFIELD ARMORY

❦

Traveling west beyond Springfield, in the direction of Albany in New York, you will find the road desolate but kept in tolerably good repair. (It's a different story for those unfortunates heading from Hartford to Albany: they're at the mercy of what one traveler, Lord Adam Gordon, calls "the worst road in America." "Ill-chosen and unfit for use and not sufficiently direct and convenient" – that's what Connecticut officials themselves have to say about this miserable, crooked byway, where fallen trees often block a traveler's way.) But note that we did use the word "desolate" – the road west of the Connecticut River enters the Berkshire Hills, a region of deep forests, occasional expansive vistas (for those who care for that sort of thing), and fierce winter storms. Villages in these hills have a look of newness about them, and for good reason: once you have ferried the Connecticut and gotten beyond Westfield, you'll find few places that have been settled for more than thirty years. Pittsfield, which lies beneath the looming bulk of Mt. Greylock, is scarcely a decade old. The threat of Indian attack, and quarrels with the colony of New York, kept Massachusetts families from making their homes here at any earlier date.

And so to New York. Beyond the border, the road continues on to Albany, the old Dutch Fort Orange, where Hollanders grew fat on the fur trade long before Great Britain took their colony for its own. If you travel this far from New England, your way to the seaport of New York will be a water route, down the great Hudson River. But that's a journey for another day, and another guidebook.

The northern route from Springfield leads through a string of pleasant valley towns. Following the course of the Connecticut River in the shadow of Mt. Tom, the road takes you in 10 miles to Northampton, settled by Connecticut families more than a century ago. It was at Northampton that the inspiring – some say terrifying – preacher Jonathan Edwards lately held the Congregational pastorate, and inspired the "Great Awakening" of religious sensibility in

Massachusetts and beyond. (Having later served as a missionary to the Indians at Stockbridge, Massachusetts, the Rev. Edwards died in 1758 while serving as the president of the College of New Jersey.)

Rev. Jonathan Edwards.

A CRADLE OF THE IVY LEAGUE

The College of New Jersey would later be renamed Princeton, after the town to which it had moved in 1756. Originally founded for the training of evangelical ministers, it abandoned its religious ties as it grew to become a major institution of higher learning.

"The people of the country, in general, I suppose, are as sober, orderly, and good sort of people, as in any part of New England ... Our being so far within the land, at a distance from sea-ports, and in a corner of the country, has doubtless been one reason why we have not been so much corrupted with vice, as most other parts."

REVEREND JONATHAN EDWARDS, FROM *A FAITHFUL NARRATIVE OF THE SURPRISING WORKS OF GOD*, 1737

Some 17 miles north of Northampton lies Deerfield, a town still saddened by the awful raid of 1704, when half the settlement was burned and about fifty of its residents killed by the French and their Indian allies (see pages 25–6).

Undaunted by these depredations, settlers returned to Deerfield in 1706. Their success in bringing the town back from the dead can be seen in handsome and now blessedly secure structures such as the home of the Sheldon family; and the Frary House, the oldest portion of which survived the raid and fire. It is today a tavern, kept by innkeeper Salah Barnard, who recently purchased it for the considerable sum of £175. After a long day's ride from Springfield, Mr. Barnard's establishment makes a convenient overnight stop – although travelers should be advised that here walks another supposed ghost, being that of one Sarah Smith, a serving-woman hung many years ago for the murder of her illegitimate child.

Into the New Hampshire Grants

The northern border of Massachusetts lies only 20 miles north of Deerfield. Now you have arrived in the New Hampshire Grants. As we mentioned earlier, the Grants' peculiar character results not only from their often forbidding mountainous terrain, but from their political status as a contention-point between New Hampshire and the colony of New York. Nevertheless, this rough frontier has attracted a hardy breed of settlers, who with remarkable steadfastness and vigor carve brave little towns out of a howling wilderness.

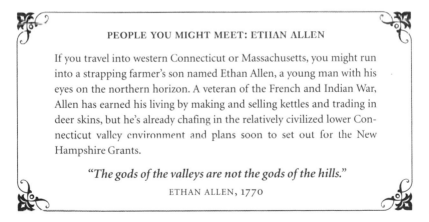

PEOPLE YOU MIGHT MEET: ETHAN ALLEN

If you travel into western Connecticut or Massachusetts, you might run into a strapping farmer's son named Ethan Allen, a young man with his eyes on the northern horizon. A veteran of the French and Indian War, Allen has earned his living by making and selling kettles and trading in deer skins, but he's already chafing in the relatively civilized lower Connecticut valley environment and plans soon to set out for the New Hampshire Grants.

"The gods of the valleys are not the gods of the hills."
ETHAN ALLEN, 1770

The first such settlement you will reach is Brattleboro, on the Connecticut River across from New Hampshire proper. Named for a Massachusetts land speculator, William Brattle, who was a part owner of the tract on which it stands but who never bothered to visit it, Brattleboro was for many years no more than the site of an outpost called Fort Dummer (after a Massachusetts governor), and has only recently been settled as a civilian community.

If you want to explore Vermont beyond Brattleboro, your travels will take you – most likely on foot, on horseback, or, on the larger rivers, by canoe – to one town after another granted by that tireless grantor, New Hampshire Governor Benning Wentworth. Many of them have yet to be populated, and those that have remain quite rustic. One that does show promise was named after the governor himself. It isn't called "Wentworth," but Bennington, and it lies 40 miles west of Brattleboro by way of a rough trail that climbs and descends the mountainous backbone of Vermont. Bennington hasn't been settled for long, but should prosper due to its location in a valley that offers easy access to Massachusetts settlements in the Berkshire Hills, and the fledgling Vermont communities to the north.

A STUBBORN MISNOMER

In August of 1777, the Battle of Bennington will be a crucial victory for the Americans in their war for independence. But the battle will actually be fought in Walloomsac, on the New York side of the border. Bennington will be the virtual capital of the Republic of Vermont, which will exist as an independent state before joining the Union in 1791.

The trail north from Bennington follows the great valley of Vermont through straggling, isolated settlements, across the forest domain of the catamount and the black bear, eventually reaching the 50-mile-long navigable portion of Otter Creek, the longest river in the Grants. If you can secure the use of a canoe, Otter Creek will take you to Lake Champlain, reached after a portage around a waterfall less than 5 miles from the lake at Panton. Long a favored route of Indian marauders, the great lake extends for over 100 miles, and forms the border between New England and New York. Paddle north along its wooded shores, past the rough new village of Burlington, and you will reach the Richelieu River and the water route, now entirely in British hands, to the St. Lawrence River, the cities of Montreal and Quebec, and the vastness of Lower Canada.

FROM WESTERN NEW ENGLAND TO THE NEW YORK BORDER

Hartford, first town of Connecticut, lies but 25 miles south from Springfield, along the Connecticut River. You might have taken a more direct route from Boston to Hartford, by following the Post Road into Connecticut by way of the Massachusetts towns of Dedham, Uxbridge, and Southbridge; but as our path lay directly west to Springfield, we will follow the river south from there.

Post roads extend south from Springfield on both sides of the river, running into Connecticut at Enfield on the eastern shore, and Suffield on the west. But you might wish to travel on the river itself, especially after you have passed the Enfield Rapids. This stretch of water denies passage to sailing vessels, though skillfully manned flatboats are used to transport goods, and the occasional intrepid passenger, south into calmer and deeper water.

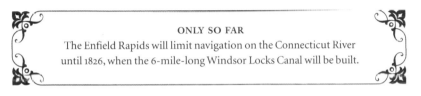

ONLY SO FAR
The Enfield Rapids will limit navigation on the Connecticut River until 1826, when the 6-mile-long Windsor Locks Canal will be built.

As you pass through the countryside just south of the Massachusetts border, you may see plantings of tobacco. Although Indians grew tobacco in the rich valley soil before the English arrived, its recent cultivation dates back only a year or two, to when Connecticut soldier Israel Putnam brought back seed – and, allegedly, "three donkey-loads of Havana seegars" – following the British raid on the Cuban capital. The big, broad leaves of tobacco may soon crowd out the valley's edible crops, as the plant seems to thrive in Connecticut soil.

Some 14 miles south of the rapids, the spires of Hartford rise above the western bank of the Connecticut. This is where Thomas Hooker and his followers from Cambridge, Massachusetts, came to settle in 1636, much to the dismay of the Dutchmen who had established a trading fort here – an outpost which they soon abandoned. Hooker's people wrote a constitution for their new colony, and commenced the meetings of what they then called their "General Court." Like Rhode Island, though, Connecticut has been wary of confining its colonial government to a single location, and so Hartford shares with New Haven the role of capital. The General Assembly, however, still meets only at Hartford.

BRIGHT FUTURES

Later renowned for his military prowess, Israel Putnam was instrumental in establishing Connecticut's profitable tobacco-growing industry.

Connecticut will indeed become famous for its superior tobacco leaves, which are used especially for the outer wrapping of cigars. As for Israel Putnam, he was to earn fame in a general's rank during the American Revolution.

Despite its inland location, Hartford is vigorously engaged in shipbuilding and seaborne trade. Hartford men own a goodly number of the Connecticut colony's sailing vessels, and the shipyards at North Meadow Creek are always busy. It is not uncommon to see goods sold directly from the decks of ships docked at Hartford's riverside wharves, or to read notices of captains soliciting cargo for transport to foreign markets.

Casual travelers likely will not be interested in ships' cargoes. But if you are fortunate to arrive at Hartford in May or September – specifically, on the second Wednesdays of those months – you will find all sorts of goods for sale at the fairs held at Market Square, in the center of town. Long a community fixture, the fairs have recently been revived.

Before pressing on to New Haven, or returning to Boston either by retracing your route to Springfield or taking the Post Road through northeastern Connecticut, you may find ample hospitality at David Bull's tavern, at the sign of the Bunch of Grapes, on Main Street opposite the State House. Just across the street, we should note, is the shop of the printer and bookseller Thomas Green, publisher with Ebenezer Watson of that lively journal the *Connecticut Courant*, and of a useful and popular almanac. (Amos Hinsdale's tavern, a short distance away at the corner of Wyllys Street, is a worthy alternative if Mr. Bull has no accommodations.)

A CONNECTICUT ICON

When in Hartford, be sure to see the Charter Oak, a huge tree of great age that is a treasure to the people of Connecticut. It was in a crevice of this mighty oak that independent-minded Hartford men hid the colony's original royal charter, to keep it safe from the tyrant Edmund Andros, who had been sent by King James II in 1684 to rule as governor of all New England. Andros never found the charter, which remained safe until the colonies' rights had been restored after the accession of King William in 1688.

New Haven, Seat of Learning

As with travel between Springfield and Hartford, the first part of the journey south from Hartford to New Haven may be made by either a land or a water route – with the advantage, should the river be your preference, of offering no such obstructions as the Enfield Rapids. But as the Post Road and the river part ways beyond Wethersfield, with the Connecticut veering southeastward towards its meeting with Long Island Sound, you may as well follow the land route from the start.

Wethersfield, 6 miles south of Hartford on the west bank of the Connecticut, rivals Hartford as a shipping center, as you can see from the size and number of its riverside warehouses (and as you can hear from the boasts of Wethersfield men in the Chester family's tavern). All sorts of local produce and manufactures are shipped from the town docks, including hats, bricks, tobacco, and an immense number of onions, for which the rich local soil is well suited.

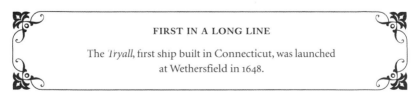

FIRST IN A LONG LINE

The *Tryall*, first ship built in Connecticut, was launched at Wethersfield in 1648.

On through Meriden, Wallingford, and North Haven the road continues, doubtless affording you the chance to meet some of Connecticut's famous "Yankee peddlers" on their native ground. The peddlers fan out each year from southern Connecticut towns such as Middletown and Berlin, with their packs bulging with all manner of household goods. It's said that the business began some twenty years ago, when two brothers named Pattison came from Ireland with a supply of tinned sheet iron and began making cups, saucers, and plates that quickly became more popular than pewter. That was the beginning of the Connecticut tinware business, which thrives today. And since articles made of tin are light and easily carried, peddling became the practical way to sell them, along with a great assortment of small items that every household needs.

A Connecticut peddler, with his donkey and his wares.

"Their sobriety is exchanged for cunning; their honesty for imposition ... No course of life tends more rapidly to eradicate every moral feeling."

YALE PRESIDENT TIMOTHY DWIGHT, CONCERNING
YOUNG MEN DRAWN TO THE PEDDLERS' TRADE

The town of New Haven, famous as a seaport and as one of New England's two great seats of learning, clusters around its harbor on Long Island Sound 40 miles south of Hartford. It is, as you will no doubt discover at the hearthside in either of the two towns, Hartford's great rival for primacy in the colony of Connecticut. New Haven is but two years younger than Hartford, having been settled in 1638 by a party of Londoners who arrived by way of Boston. They were led by the Reverend John Davenport, a fanatically strict Puritan divine.

New Haven remained its own colony – or, rather, Rev. Davenport's colony – until 1664, when it merged with the rest of Connecticut, and even by the standards of our ancestors it was a place known for the rigidity of its laws: in place of English Common Law, the rules of the Old Testament held sway, and a child over the age of sixteen could be put to death for cursing or striking his parent. Fortunately, the threat of encroachment by the colony of New York led New Haven into its eventual merger with the then Hartford-led colony. Should you happen to be a Quaker, you no longer need fear branding and banishment if your travels take you to New Haven.

～ぶ～

"No woman shall kiss her child on the Sabbath or Fasting Days."

"No one shall travel, make beds, cook, sweep house, shave, or cut hair on the Sabbath."

"No one shall read the common prayer, keep Christmas or Saints Days, make minced pies, dance, play cards, or play on any instrument of music except it be the drum, trumpet, or a Jewsharp."

A SELECTION OF THE SO-CALLED "BLUE LAWS" OF THE COLONY OF NEW HAVEN, AS PUBLISHED BY THE REVEREND SAMUEL PETERS IN 1781. SOME CHARGE THAT REV. PETERS, A MINISTER OF THE CHURCH OF ENGLAND, MISREPRESENTED MANY OF THE EARLY LAWS IN ORDER TO CAST RIDICULE ON THE PURITANS

～ぐ～

New Haven grew up around its Green, which is still the central feature of the town's tidy grid of streets and squares. Here, near where the first meeting-house was built, stands the present State House and County Court. But for many present and former residents of the town, its true heart is the square bounded by Chapel, High, Elm, and College streets. This has been the home of Yale College (see page 117) since it was moved here from Saybrook in 1716. The college's oldest building has stood here since 1717, and nearby is its newest, Connecticut Hall, built barely a decade ago in 1752. Much was made, in the early days of this institution, of its role as a counter to Harvard College, where

New Haven's Yale College. The college chapel is on the left.

educational rigor and theological orthodoxy were seen to have become neg-
lected. The two institutions lately have been less stringently opposed, however,
and we doubt that any serious rivalry between them will persist in the future.

Especially if you have made the trip from Hartford to New Haven in a single day, you will be ready for a night's rest at the snug tavern opened in 1760 by
Mr. Nathan Beers, on the Green at the corner of College and Chapel streets.
This is New Haven's foremost hostelry, and is frequently chosen as the site for
public dinners.

A CHARMED LOCATION

The tradition of hospitality begun by Nathan Beers and his son, Isaac, will continue at the corner of College and Chapel streets for two and a half centuries. In the 1850s, a hotel called the New Haven House will be erected on the site. This will be demolished in 1910 to make way for the Taft Hotel. In 2009, a splendid new restaurant will advertise as having occupied the Taft's former ballroom.

Along Connecticut's Southeastern Coast

New Haven is the place in which all of the various routes leading from Boston to New York meet and become one road, known as the King's Highway. If you have traveled to New England from New York or points south, this will be your way home – unless, of course, you are taking ship from New Haven. Likewise, it will be the route to follow if you are interested in visiting the remaining Connecticut towns that line the shores of Long Island Sound.

The King's Highway leads through level terrain, undistinguished by any scenic prospects save an occasional glimpse of the Sound. At Stratford, about 15 miles west of New Haven, you must cross the broad mouth of the Housatonic River by ferry. The first of these boats was operated by Moses Wheeler, who at the time of his death in 1698 was one hundred years old, and is said to have been the first man in these colonies to reach that great age. Not nearly so ancient, but still the oldest of its kind in Connecticut, is the colony's first Anglican church, built in 1723.

Stratfield, 5 miles farther west, is gathered about the mouth of the Pequonnock River. Here you must make another ferry crossing, although the Pequonnock is not nearly so wide as the Housatonic. Fortify yourself for the short voyage with a stop at the Pixlee Tavern, on North Street just before the river, where the fried local oysters are excellent.

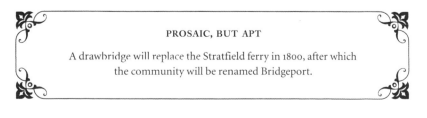

PROSAIC, BUT APT

A drawbridge will replace the Stratfield ferry in 1800, after which the community will be renamed Bridgeport.

The next sizable town along the King's Highway is Fairfield, where the Mill River makes necessary yet another ferry crossing. As much of a nuisance as this may be for the traveler, the river opens into a fine harbor at Southport, where the protection of an offshore reef makes this one of the more tranquil havens for shipping along the Connecticut coast. We can recommend a stop at Samuel Penfield's tavern, on the Town Green; though as we have not tried them, we cannot vouch for the quality of his oysters. But the creatures are plentiful and delicious at Norwalk, where the fishery is a major local industry – and where, we are at pains to report, yet another ferry crossing is required – this one at the Silvermine River.

Between Norwalk and Stamford, a distance of about 10 miles, there lies a dreary stretch called the Peat Swamp. Here we must digress from our earlier assurance that the post roads of New England are free of highwaymen, as it is not unknown here for robbers to set upon unwary travelers and even carriers of the mail. These occurrences are by no means frequent, although we would be remiss in failing to offer a warning.

Along the way from Stamford to Greenwich, it is the terrain rather than the criminal element that might give pause to the traveler. All the way to the New York border, the King's Highway is subject to rocky defiles and steep descents; and proceeding on foot or on a nimble mount is less nerve-wracking, here, than in any sort of wheeled conveyance. For variety, there is yet another ferry, to be boarded at the Mianus River.

Greenwich marks the southwestern end of Connecticut, and of New England as well. One might well look at a map and wonder why the colony extends even this far along the Sound, as an odd little westward handle appears to have been added to Connecticut at the clear expense of New York. But this geographical quirk was the result of a compromise, agreed upon in 1683, which assured the larger colony a north-south boundary 20 miles east of the Hudson River, in return for allowing Greenwich and Stamford to remain a part of Connecticut.

So here New England creeps close to its great lively neighbor, maintaining still a decorous distance from that old Dutch harbor at the Hudson's mouth. It is, some say, a distance of more than mere miles.

VI

ACCOMMODATIONS, FOOD, AND DRINK

PUTTING UP FOR THE NIGHT

C onsider yourself fortunate if you have acquaintances you can stay with when visiting New England. In cities as well as outlying towns, inns and taverns offer a rudimentary sort of accommodation, with small consideration for privacy, and it's not uncommon for an innkeeper to crowd two or more beds into each of his drafty upstairs rooms (a fire, if there's a hearth in your room, will entail an extra charge). As one British army officer commented after touring New England, "The general custom of having two or three beds in a room to be sure is very disagreeable; it arises from the great increase in travelling within the last few years, and the smallness of their houses, which were not built for houses of entertainment."

A tavern welcomes mariners to Salem's harbor in this silk-embroidered scene.

If two or three beds to a room were too much for this fastidious traveler, we can only imagine his reaction to the typical New England practice of assigning two guests to the same bed. It doesn't matter if the pair are complete strangers – even after you've gone to sleep, your innkeeper might show up, with his candlestick in his hand and a newly arrived lodger in tow. The stranger is shown to your bed, and you can only hope that he takes his boots off, doesn't snore too loudly, and has bathed sometime since the last coronation.

Not that we blame the landlord: why should he get only three or four pence from the use of one of his beds for the night, when he might double that amount? (He might even triple it, by tucking three travelers into a bed.)

That said, a good New England inn (the term is interchangeable with tavern, when such institutions offer overnight lodgings) can be a pleasant place indeed in the hours before bedtime. With New England's weather what it is for half the year, who could have anything to say against the welcome offered by a cozy taproom, with a fire blazing on the hearth?

The key to an inn's hospitality, of course, is the landlord, and these individuals come from one of the best-praised classes of citizens in New England. In the earliest days of these colonies, the men licensed to keep taverns were handpicked by local authorities. "Every innkeeper in Connecticut," one writer recalled, "must be recommended by the selectmen and civil authorities, constables and grand jurors of the town in which he resides."

Things have loosened up considerably in our day, and townsmen aren't in the habit of handpicking tavern keepers as if they were interviewing ministers, but your landlord is still liable to be one of the more upstanding members of the community – "in general," in the words of a recent traveler in New England, "well informed and well behaved ... with respect to situation and intelligence, he is at least on a level with the generality of his visitors." You might even find the selectmen of a town holding their regular meetings at a favorite tavern, with the landlord joining right in their deliberations.

"You will find the house [tavern] full of people drinking drams, flip, toddy, carousing, swearing, but especially plotting with the landlord to get him at the next town meeting an election either for selectman or representative."

JOHN ADAMS, 1761

By nature a talkative and inquisitive lot, landlords can occasionally bedevil a traveler with a bit too much inquiry. We're reminded of what Benjamin Franklin claims is his standard recitation whenever he stops at an inn: "My name is Benjamin Franklin. I was born in Boston. I am a printer by profession, am traveling to Philadelphia, shall have to return at such a time, and have no news. Now, what can you give me for dinner?" Mr. Franklin must know by now, though, that any landlord worth his salt must take this supposed conversation-stopper as a challenge to come up with a whole new line of questioning.

~ ⊙⊙ ~

"As to landlord, he is as happy and as big, as proud, as conceited, as any nobleman in England, always calm and good-natured and lazy, but the contemplation of his farm and his sons, his house and pasture and cows, his sound judgment as he thinks, and his great holiness as well as that of his wife, keep him as erect in his thoughts as a noble or a prince."

JOHN ADAMS, DESCRIBING HIS HOST AT THE IPSWICH INN

~ ⊙⊙ ~

From the Colonies' Ample Larder

The New England colonies have come a long way from the days when the Pilgrim settlers of Plymouth would have perished of starvation during their first winter, had the Indians not shared their stored harvest of maize and beans. Over the past century and a half, New Englanders have proven themselves industrious and successful farmers. The crops cultivated by the Indians are now our staples, along with wheat, barley, apples, and other familiar foods brought here from Britain. What of our fierce long winters, and the shortness of our growing season? In the countryside, produce such as apples, turnips, potatoes, onions, parsnips, pumpkins, and winter squashes are kept beneath layers of hay in stone-lined excavations called root cellars, where they are preserved against freezing. Beans are dried, and baked with molasses and salt pork in iron vessels set in the embers on the great kitchen hearths that stand at the center of every New England dwelling.

Apple

nip

Parsnip

Onion

The fruits and vegetables that form the mainstay of the colonists' diet are supplemented by meat from those animals that can be cheaply raised, with pork always a favorite – the amount of land needed for grazing cattle makes beef a luxury , although cows are kept for milking, and oxen are far more common than horses as farmers' beasts of burden. The meat of hogs slaughtered in autumn is salted and dried, or preserved in brine to carry through the winter. Wild game, though not so plentiful near larger towns and cities as it was in the early days of settlement, is still abundant in the countryside. Deer, hare, partridge, turkey, and even bear fall to New England hunters, providing fresh meat during the long winters. The farther into the back reaches of New England you travel, the more likely it is that the fare at your inn will include this provender of the forest.

Pork, smoked or cured in brine, sees many colonists through the winter.

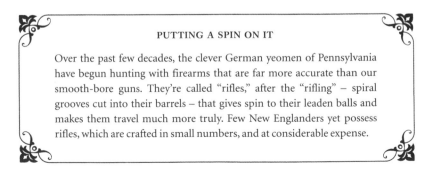

PUTTING A SPIN ON IT

Over the past few decades, the clever German yeomen of Pennsylvania have begun hunting with firearms that are far more accurate than our smooth-bore guns. They're called "rifles," after the "rifling" – spiral grooves cut into their barrels – that gives spin to their leaden balls and makes them travel much more truly. Few New Englanders yet possess rifles, which are crafted in small numbers, and at considerable expense.

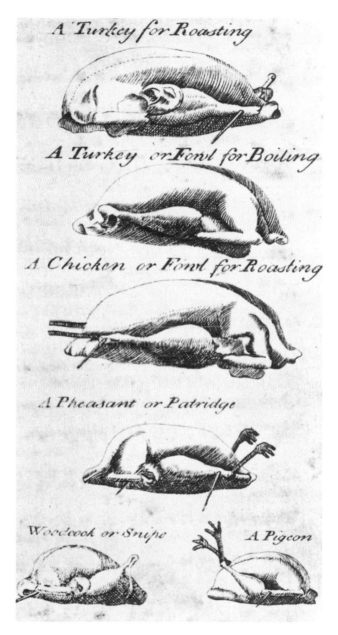

Paul Revere's engravings for The Frugal Housewife, *a cookery book.*

Maize, so named to distinguish it from the other grains called "corn" in Britain, is dried and ground for use in the porridge known as "Indian pudding." Flavored with molasses (or, farther from the coast, the syrup made from boiling the sap of maple trees) and served at all meals of the day, Indian pudding bakes on New England hearths in all seasons.

A NEW ENGLAND TREAT

If you've enjoyed a bowl of Indian pudding at an inn or private home during your travels in New England, you might want to try making it at your own hearthside. Here's a popular recipe: stir a handful of corn meal into a quart of scalded milk, and add half a cup of molasses and a half teaspoon of salt. If you can afford rare spices from the East Indies, a bit of nutmeg and cinnamon will help flavor your dish. Set your pudding bowl in a pan of hot water, and place the pan close to the coals in your hearth. You've no need to stir, and your pudding should be ready in three hours. If this is too long to wait, you can make a simple "hasty pudding" by stirring cornmeal into boiling water and turning with a spoon until your porridge has thickened.

Cod, haddock, pollock, and mackerel abound in in- and offshore waters, and clams and oysters are plentiful. Much of the catch – especially of codfish and clams – finds its way into chowder, a hearty soup made of layers of salt pork, hard ships' biscuit, onions, potatoes, and fish (or the chopped meat of the fist-sized quahog clams), then simmered with water and milk or cream. If you're spending the night at an inn near the seacoast, you're likely to be welcomed with a bowl of chowder, or perhaps a serving of clam or oyster pie. Lobsters, though abundant, are considered fit only for the poor, and it will be a humble lodging indeed where a lobster will be set upon the table.

Freshwater fish, especially salmon and shad, are trapped in nets and weirs at the time of their migration up the great rivers of New England, such as the Connecticut, Merrimack, and Piscataqua.

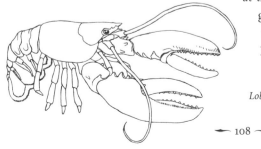

Lobsters are plentiful, but held in small regard.

NEW ENGLAND'S POWERFUL THIRST

The common drinks of New England are cider and beer. Cider, made from the autumn harvest of apples and lightly fermented, is drunk by adults and children alike – it's not uncommon for a New Englander to quaff a quart at breakfast alone. A far stronger drink, called applejack, is sometimes made by placing a lidless keg of cider outdoors overnight in freezing weather, and drawing off the liquor that lies beneath the ice formed by water rising to the top. Repeated several times – until no more ice forms – this method yields a powerful potion, sure to intoxicate. It's best left to the orchardmen of New Jersey, a British colony still well populated by the free-tippling Dutch, where it is made in great quantities. (Even farther south, and in the Appalachian hills, the Scotch-Irish emigrants know how to distill a man-felling potion out of barley or rye – or, heaven help us, Indian corn. The less said of *that*, the better.)

Beer or ale, made from the fermented mash of barley, is drunk as commonly in the colonies as it is in England, and your innkeeper will likely be a brewer as well. The first enterprise set up by the Pilgrim settlers was a brewery, as beer has always been considered a more healthful drink than water.

"Oh we can make liquor to sweeten our lips
Of pumpkins, of parsnips, of walnut-tree chips."

FROM AN OLD SONG, CELEBRATING NEW ENGLANDERS'
INVENTIVENESS IN BREWING AND DISTILLING

Among the wealthier classes, and in the finer city taverns, wines imported from Europe are highly prized. The most popular by far is the fortified wine from the Portuguese island of Madeira, which is drunk with meals by the pint by those who can afford this next step up from beer and cider. Wines without the lashing of brandy that gives Madeira and port their potency are much more likely to spoil on the long sea voyage to New England, unless they are shipped in bottles stoppered with cork, a clever Spanish and Portuguese innovation.

Even stronger, and sure not to spoil, is brandy itself, the "burnt wine" – but New Englanders wishing a drink more powerful than cider, beer, or wine are

Pleased with pipe and punch: an over-mantel painting in Sturbridge, Massachusetts.

generally happy with rum, made right here in our colonies from molasses distilled on the sugar plantations of Jamaica, Barbados, and the smaller islands of Britain's great Caribbean empire.

It's rum, after all, that stiffens the spine of two of New England's favorite drinks – flip and punch, both tavern standbys. We've already taken a look (on page 12) at the flip Mr. Ezekiel Howe serves at his Red Horse Tavern in Sudbury, Massachusetts, but it's worth noting that most flip recipes call for adding rum to sugar- or molasses-sweetened beer, not milk, and then heating the concoction with a red-hot iron "flip-dog" or fire poker.

Punch is a more complex and festive drink. A typical recipe might call for water, sugar, the juice of fresh lemons, and rum, seasoned with a dusting of ground nutmeg. Lemons – or the alternative limes or oranges – are along with nutmeg the items of greatest rarity and expense in a good punch, and Boston tavern-keepers make a dash to Mr. J. Crosby's shop, The Box of Lemons, whenever a ship arrives from tropical seas, bringing him a consignment of these perishable luxuries.

A PURITAN'S PUNISHMENT

While public intoxication is still frowned upon in New England, attitudes toward over-imbibing have softened considerably since 1644, when one Robert Coles of Roxbury was forced to wear a red letter "D" on a white cloth background around his neck for a year, after his conviction of the crime of drunkenness. We've heard of such a punishment for adultery, but imposing the "Scarlet D" sentence was going to extremes!

New England's city dwellers have enjoyed their coffeehouses for nearly a century, ever since the first one opened in Boston in 1670. Coffee is a popular drink among the upper classes and, if rumors of a future parliamentary tax on tea are to be believed, the once-exotic Turkish brew formerly reviled as "syrup of soot" and "essence of old shoes" might become the standard beverage of all social orders.

But even in fashionable coffeehouses, you'll find most patrons enjoying an alcoholic tipple. It just doesn't seem right to drink the king's health – or the health of his American critics, if that's your preference – in anything that doesn't pack at least a bit of a kick.

A

Coffee-Houfe,

Is opened by WILLIAM RICHARDS in Middletown, at the Sign of the fpread Eagle, where he hopes the Attention to Cuftomers, may be honored with their Approbation.

Newspaper advertisement for a Connecticut coffee house.

VII

RELIGION, EDUCATION, THE PRESS, AND THE POST

THE ROLE OF RELIGION

On any given Sunday, you're likely to find more than three-quarters of New Englanders attending church services. This shouldn't be too surprising in a place founded by staunch believers – but the big difference between today's religious landscape and the old Puritan heyday is the growing diversity of sects and beliefs.

Although Presbyterianism has made some inroads, Congregationalism is still New England's number one denomination, with its familiar stark, unornamented meetinghouses at the center of town and town life. But to the horror of the old school Puritans who created the Congregational establishment, the Church of England finally got a foothold here during the governorship of the hated Edmund Andros, who established Boston's King's Chapel in 1686. Whether you're an Anglican communicant or not, be sure to visit the congregation's new home, a handsome granite structure (the stone was quarried in nearby Quincy) just erected in 1754 in the latest neoclassical style. (The burying ground next to the chapel, by the way, is a good deal older, and anything but Anglican in its origins – John Winthrop, Massachusetts' first governor, is buried there, and the staunch old Puritan must roll in his grave when the bell tolls for Sunday services).

Old Ship Meeting House, Hingham, Massachusetts.

> ## ANGLICAN EXTRAVAGANCE
>
> In 1713, the original King's Chapel became the first church
> in New England to acquire an organ.

Outside the cities, you aren't likely to find all that many Church of England adherents, nor will you run into more than the occasional Deist. Deism is more of an urban and upper-class phenomenon, an intellectual's religion (if it can be called that) disdainful of the idea of a personal God and dismissive of Christ's divinity. At quite the other extreme, though, you'll find many New Englanders still caught up in the enthusiasm of the "Great Awakening," that groundswell of evangelical enthusiasm that reached its peak in the 1740s when English preacher George Whitefield and our own Jonathan Edwards shouted out the need for all to accept Christ as their personal savior, and thundered home the message that faith, not good works, was the key to salvation. Spend a few months in New England, and you'll no doubt meet a number of citizens who claim to have heard the late Reverend Edwards deliver his famous sermon, "Sinners in the Hands of an Angry God" at Enfield, Connecticut. (You may meet more of these folks than could have fit into the church, but maybe they read the sermon. Either way, it probably scared them out of their wits.)

"The God that holds you over the pit of hell, much as one holds
a spider, or some detestable insect, over the fire, detests you, and
is dreadfully provoked: His wrath towards you burns like fire;
He looks upon you as worthy of nothing else, but to be thrown into
the fire; He eyes are too pure than to bear to have you in His sight;
you are ten thousand times more abominable in His eyes,
than the most hateful venomous snake is in ours.
You have offended Him infinitely more than ever a stubborn
rebel did his prince: and yet, it is nothing but His hand
that holds you from falling into the fire every moment."

REVEREND JONATHAN EDWARDS,
"SINNERS IN THE HANDS OF AN ANGRY GOD," 1741

Quakers at meeting, in their characteristic plain clothes.

When it comes to religion in New England, little Rhode Island is the odd man out. It was founded, remember, by that great enthusiast for freedom of religion, Roger Williams, and it certainly lives up to his ideals. Here you'll find New England's one great concentration of Quakers, a denomination once so persecuted in Massachusetts that its adherents were hung on Boston Common. There are a fair number of Quakers in Newport, which is ironic since they are noted opponents of slavery. The slave trade, as you may remember, is a cornerstone of that city's prosperity.

Rhode Island also harbors New England's only Jewish community. Like the Quakers, they are concentrated in Newport, where they have recently built a fine synagogue that they've named after their congregation's leader, Isaac Touro. The Newport Jews, descendants of emigrants from Holland and its Caribbean island dependencies, are among only 1,500 of their kind in the American colonies.

One thing is certain, though: you won't find any Roman Catholics in New England. The papists are all down in Maryland.

PLACING A PREMIUM ON EDUCATION

One of New England's proudest boasts is that nearly all of its men – and most of its women – can read and write, beyond the simple skill of signing their own names. We can thank our Puritan forebears for this accomplishment, since they believed that every Christian should be able to read the Bible. In today's New England, that's not all they read – so wherever you travel in these colonies, you'll find folks who devour newspapers, British magazines, and pamphlets on the issues of the day, and who know what they're talking about in the taprooms and parlors where those issues are debated.

For nearly a century, all of the New England colonies except Rhode Island have made basic schooling a requirement for every young male. If a town has a hundred families, it has a school, and larger communities have several, all supported by taxes. These "grammar schools" teach the catechism, Latin, and mathematics, and are open only to boys (girls are taught to read at home). Such universal schooling for male children is a point of pride in New England, and the southern colonies' practice of educating their privileged young at home, with private tutors, and their poorer citizens not at all, is looked down on.

The oldest and finest of New England's training schools for college is the Boston Latin School, founded in 1635. It's expected that the young graduates of Boston Latin, like the most promising students from throughout the colonies, will head directly to New England's oldest and proudest place of higher education, Harvard College. Harvard was established at New Town, soon after named Cambridge, by order of the Great and General Court of Massachusetts in 1636. It got its name two years later, when a young Charlestown minister named John Harvard died and left the college his library of 400 books and half of his estate, amounting to £779.

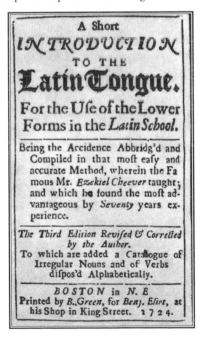

A Short
INTRODUCTION
TO THE
Latin Tongue.

For the Use of the Lower
Forms in the *Latin School*.

Being the Accidence Abbridg'd and Compiled in that moft eafy and accurate Method, wherein the Famous Mr. *Ezekiel Cheever* taught; and which he found the moft advantageous by *Seventy* years experience.

The Third Edition Revifed & Corrected by the Author.
To which are added a Catalogue of Irregular Nouns and of Verbs difpos'd Alphabetically.

BOSTON in *N. E*
Printed by *B. Green*, for *Benj. Eliot*, at his Shop in King Street. 1 7 2 4.

Latin is a cornerstone of higher education in New England.

A RECENT TRAGIC CONFLAGRATION

Nearly all of John Harvard's books were lost, along with the rest of the college's 5,000-volume library, in a fire that destroyed Harvard Hall on a winter night in 1764.

A Prospect of the Colledges in Cambridge in New England

College buildings in Harvard Yard, Cambridge.

From its beginning, Harvard's purpose was to educate the Puritan ministry, and it wasn't until 1708 that a layman was elected president. Although they're still given a solid background in theology – including even instruction in Hebrew – the Harvard students of today are no longer expected to head directly to the Congregational pulpit, and are taught the natural sciences along with logic and rhetoric. Some say the college has become altogether too worldly – decide for yourself, if you're spending time in and around Boston, by ferrying across the Charles River to Charlestown, and taking a pleasant walk of a bit more than 2 miles to the college yard, across from Cambridge Common. Here you might strike up a conversation with students and professors, and visit the handsome Massachusetts Hall, built in 1720, and the more recently constructed Holden Chapel. Hollis Hall, a new dormitory, was completed in 1763.

CROSSING THE CHARLES

The ferry from Boston to Charlestown was first operated in 1631.
It would finally be replaced by the first bridge across the Charles,
a 1,500-foot span built in 1786.

Harvard's Connecticut Rival

Harvard was New England's only college until 1701, when ten clergymen met to found a "Collegiate School" in Saybrook, Connecticut. The reason? The learned and very conservative divines had decided that Harvard's curriculum had already become too liberal. The college was moved to New Haven in 1716, and, like its Cambridge rival, was soon named after a benefactor – in this case, a wealthy former governor of the British East India Company named Elihu Yale. Along with a sum of money, his gift consisted of some 400 books and a portrait of King George I.

Harvard and Yale remain New England's only two colleges. But a Reverend James Manning is seeking to secure a charter for a "College of Rhode Island" to be run by his Baptist sect although open to members of other denominations as well, in the spirit of that colony's religious tolerance.

HUMBLE BEGINNINGS

Rev. Manning's "College of Rhode Island" was chartered in 1764 and
was also later named for a generous supporter. He was a 1783 graduate
of the college, by the name of Nicholas Brown.

NEWSPAPERS AND MAGAZINES

You won't find nearly as many magazines available in New England as there are in Britain, or even in the colonies of New York and Pennsylvania. Most such ventures fail after only a few issues. But ships arriving from England regularly carry issues of the latest London journals, which are eagerly awaited by the reading public. If you come across a copy more than a couple of days old at a popular tavern – at the Royal Exchange, say, on Boston's State Street – it probably will be dog-eared and hopelessly ale-stained.

One of the most popular of the overseas periodicals is the *Gentleman's Magazine*, published in London since 1731. There's a curious motto on the title page of each yearly special issue (which brings together the best articles from the previous twelve months): the Latin phrase *E Pluribus Unum*, meaning "out of many, one." A number of the more forward-thinking Bostonians – some would call them dreamers, or even radicals – have suggested that this might be a slogan under which the colonies could unite against perceived British injustices. Most New Englanders, though, recognize the tired old Latinism for what it is – a magazine motto. They know that they're Massachusetts men, and Rhode Islanders, and Connecticut and New Hampshiremen – and never mind their distant cousins in the faraway Carolinas. Out of many, one? One what?

Newspapers are a different story. New England has been flooded with them since the beginning of this century, when – the year was 1704 – the Boston postmaster John Campbell printed the very first issue of his *Boston News-Letter*.

NO FREEDOM FOR THIS PRESS

The *Boston News-Letter* wasn't the very first New England newspaper. That distinction went to *Publick Occurrences Both Forreign and Domestick*, published by Benjamin Harris in 1690. It ran for exactly one issue, after which the biggest publick occurrence in Harris's life was his being clapped into the pillory for publishing a newspaper without government authority.

The *News-Letter* is still published. Nowadays, it's under the capable editorship of Mr. John Draper, who each week gives us four pages of information from near and far. The first page contains mostly British and foreign news, with local doings chronicled inside. One clever recent scheme promoted by Mr. Draper in his paper was a lottery, with 6,000 tickets offered at $2 apiece. The purpose was to pave a road in Charlestown, a $1200 expense. The rest of the money was given as prizes – first prize, $750 – an extravagance that would have scandalized our Puritan ancestors.

Other Boston newspapers include the *Boston Evening Post*, which amply covers local events and bends over backwards to avoid taking sides on any issue, and the *Boston Post-Boy and Advertiser*, a

James Franklin's New England Courant.

stalwart supporter of British government policy. Ride the post roads beyond the metropolis, and you'll find copies of such journals as the *New Hampshire Gazette Weekly*, the *Newport Mercury*, the *New London Summary*, and the *Hartford Courant*, all more or less current, depending on how recently the latest stage has stopped at your inn.

One newspaper that older readers miss is the *New England Courant*, which a young man names James Franklin started in 1721 and published for six years. Franklin didn't just print stale news from abroad and the texts of politicians' speeches. Right on the front page, he ran thoughtful essays in the then-popular style of Addison and Steele's London *Spectator*, and filled his pages with humorous and satirical letters from imaginary correspondents. Some of the *Courant*'s cleverest essays were, unknown to James, contributed by his teenage brother, Benjamin, who wrote under the name of "Silence Dogood." When young Ben Franklin left his native Boston for Philadelphia, where he has prospered as a printer, civic leader, and dabbler in the sciences, New England lost one of its most original thinkers. Nearing sixty, Mr. Franklin has showed no signs of slowing down – and as you'll see below, he now has yet another hat to wear.

*"My brother had, in 1720 or 1721, begun to print a newspaper.
It was the second to appear in America, and was called the*
New England Courant. *The only one before it was the* Boston
News-Letter. *I remember his being dissuaded by some of
his friends from the undertaking, as not likely to succeed,
one newspaper being, in their judgment,
enough for America."*

THE AUTOBIOGRAPHY OF BENJAMIN FRANKLIN, 1771–90

GETTING OUT THE NEWS

When you think of the difficulties involved in printing and distributing newspapers in New England, it's a wonder they're available at all. Paper is made from rags, which are in short supply in the colonies (some snobbish British detractors might say that this is because the colonists are wearing them!), so paper is mostly imported from abroad. Presses are simple wooden devices, on which type must be set and ink applied by hand, and printers have to use quite a bit of muscle to operate the levers and screws that bring paper and type together.

The next task is to get the papers into readers' hands. This isn't much of a problem in the larger cities and towns, where boys can carry copies to vendors and subscribers, but delivering the news to smaller settlements and outlying districts has to be left to post-boys on horseback, and stagecoach drivers. It's no wonder that only the most successful newspapers have circulations of more than 600 copies – or that the news, once it reaches some isolated country village, is about as fresh as a codfish sent the same way.

POSTAL SERVICES

The American colonies have had a system for delivering mail almost since they were first settled. New Englanders are proud of the fact that they were the first to have a colonial post office, though we're using the term a little loosely. By an order of the Massachusetts General Court issued in 1639, mail arriving from Britain had to be delivered to the Boston home of one Richard Fairbanks, who was charged with delivering it to its destination and paid a penny for each letter that passed through his hands.

The young Benjamin Franklin, an anonymous contributor to his brother's Courant.

The time is long past when the colonial mails could pile up on one man's kitchen table. New England, like all of Britain's North American colonies, now boasts a professional postal service, with regular routes and rates. One big reason behind recent improvements is the Crown's 1753 appointment of just the right man for the job of deputy postmaster general in charge of the northern colonies: Benjamin Franklin. In his first year in office, Franklin spent ten weeks traveling around New England with a contraption called an "odometer," calculating the exact mileages along the post roads, and placing markers at every mile. This helped town postmasters figure postage rates, which was important since charges – set by the legislatures in each colony – are based on distance, and patrons loved to argue over just how far their letters had to travel.

The mails are carried by postriders, who head out from the cities and larger towns when they have enough mail to cover their travel expenses. The riders take the main post roads as much as they can, and once off these beaten paths they make their way by whatever trails are passable. Travelers can thus be assured that although their correspondence won't be delivered according to an exact timetable, it will eventually get where it's going. As for mail bound for Britain and the continent, however, delivery necessarily depends on the erratic schedules of ship departures and the speed of the Atlantic crossing.

VIII

SHOPPING

When you're ready to head home, make sure to reserve space in your coach or ship's hold for some examples of American craftsmanship. Tell your friends that you picked up a few pieces of silver or furniture in New England, and they'll wonder when your taste started running to the rustic. But gone are the days when settlers living hand-to-mouth carved wooden plates and spoons, and imported just about everything else. When folks on the other side of the Atlantic see your new treasures, they'll marvel at New England artistry – and regret the extra money they've spent at high-class shops in London or on the continent. You'll be equally surprised if you're visiting from the southern or West Indian colonies, where fine craftsmanship has been slower to develop due to wealthier patrons' preference for importing their furniture and housewares from Britain.

SILVER AND PEWTER

Don't leave Boston without stopping at the home and workshop of New England's finest silversmith, Paul Revere. Look for a small wooden house – smaller each year, with Revere's growing family – on North Square, just before Prince Street if you're walking toward the harbor. You'll probably find Revere at his workbench, unless he's popped out to a tavern to talk politics. And even if he's working, he'll probably find time to tell whoever's listening what he

Paul Revere's home and workshop, Boston.

thinks of the British Parliament's latest insults to the colonies. Let it go in one ear and out the other – you're there for the silver, not the silversmith's opinions on the Stamp Act or the tea monopoly.

PEOPLE YOU MIGHT MEET: PAUL REVERE

Paul Revere, just home from the wars against the French and Indians, apprenticed under his father to learn the craft of silversmithing (the elder Revere, in his turn, apprenticed under the great John Coney). As the years go by, he will be recognized as one of New England's greatest artisans; and along the way he'll dabble in trades as diverse as printmaking and crafting false teeth. Eventually, he will run a lucrative bell foundry and copper sheathing business – but he'll be remembered by history for his ride of April 18, 1775, warning the townspeople of Middlesex County of advancing British troops.

Tea? If that's your drink, Revere will sell you a charming little teapot, like the one he's holding in his portrait by John Singleton Copley (see Plate VII), for £10 16s. 8d. – try topping that in London. If that's a little steep for steeping tea leaves, you might want to consider a creampot, priced at £2 2s. 3d., or a matched pair of porringers for £1 6s. 8d. But if you're really in a mood to splurge, and if tea isn't your drink anyway, a coffeepot in Revere's best rococo style will set you back £17. That's a bit more than an entire year's rent for a modest Boston house, but a lot less than you'll pay back home.

Smart shoppers are saying that the time to stock up on Revere silver is now, before this radical craftsman gets so consumed by politics that he puts down his hammers and takes up his political engravings full time. And if Boston's political kettle really boils over, Paul Revere is more likely to be dashing about, taking up some alarmist hue and cry, than working his magic with silver in that little house on North Square. But who knows? If Revere's politics bring him fame, for good or ill, then you may be delighted to own even a small example of his prodigious output – sugar tongs, say, or even a set of buttons or a pair of shoe buckles. Or how about a set of six teaspoons?

A Revere coffeepot.

At present, the price is only 9s. – cheap, when you think of what might be their future conversation value. "Those?" you can tell your guests as they stir their tea, "Those were made by Paul Revere."

FINE FURNITURE

The region's furniture makers have also been crafting quite a reputation. Good hardwoods may be getting hard to come by in the British Isles, but New England has abundant supplies of maple, chestnut, and cherry, and enjoys ready access to mahogany from Britain's Caribbean possessions. Skilled artisans throughout these colonies, especially in Newport, Rhode Island, and Portsmouth, New Hampshire, are adept at taking this superb stock of raw material and turning it into exquisite chests, highboys, desks, dining tables, and chairs (for this last item, look into the fine work done by the Gaines family of Portsmouth).

Newport's furniture craftsmen have been in the forefront of eschewing painted or veneer woods in their pieces in favor of solid mahogany. If you're visiting the Rhode Island capital, make an appointment to see John Townsend, a cabinetmaker with a special knack for embellishing his work with carving. Townsend is a master at creating ball-and-claw feet for his tables and chairs, and is known for his signature "block and shell" and foliage motifs on desks and chests of drawers (see Plate VIII). Other outstanding pieces by this superb craftsman include high chests set upon graceful cabriole legs, exquisite card tables, and larger drop-leaf dining tables.

In recent years, John Townsend has also been making handsome cases for tall standing clocks, with works provided by the ingenious mechanics who have lately taken up that craft in neighboring Connecticut. If the piece you want isn't in stock, Townsend will be happy to take special orders and ship. And unlike most American cabinetmakers, Mr. Townsend signs and dates his work. As his fame increases, so will the value of your piece.

Chair by John Gaines III, Portsmouth.

Vanity – and a Good Investment

If vanity gets the best of you – or if you want a truly personal gift for a special someone back home – why not have your portrait painted? The man to see is John Singleton Copley, a young Bostonian who ranks as the best portraitist in the colonies. We met him just above, as the artist who captured Paul Revere in his shirtsleeves, a thoughtful expression on his face and a teapot in his hand. Copley also did a terrific job with his remarkably true-to-life painting of wealthy merchant Nicholas Boylston in a green silk dressing gown (that gown was an import; you still can't buy anything quite that posh from a New England tailor), and with an amusing study of young Henry Pelham holding his pet squirrel on a little golden chain that was crafted by none other than Paul Revere. Copley, who lives up near the Hancock mansion on the shoulder of Beacon Hill, will gladly arrange for a sitting, although his

Copley's Boy With a Squirrel.

work doesn't come cheap – after all, he commands the princely income of 300 guineas a year, all of it from his activities as a portraitist. Now is the time to take advantage of his talent, before he starts commanding an even higher price – which he's sure to do, especially if he abandons Boston and moves to London, as he's been talking about doing ever since Bostonians have begun chafing under Parliament's latest laws. Copley has no interest in politics – and his wife's family runs the tea monopoly, which doesn't sit well with the locals.

A REAL ESTATE TIP

When revolution breaks out in 1775, John Singleton Copley will indeed leave Boston for London. His Beacon Hill property, meanwhile, will be expropriated, and developed into an upper-class residential neighborhood as soon as the war is over. We wouldn't be surprised if, someday, "Beacon Hill" is Boston's best address.

TRUE NATIVE CRAFTSMANSHIP

For truly unique gifts or souvenirs of your travels, consider acquiring examples of the artisanry of New England's surviving native Indians. For countless
generations, the tribes have been crafting necessary items out of materials
found in their woodland homes. And while modern American and European
manufactures might be more practical for our everyday use, the natives' work
has an exotic appeal that goes beyond mere utilitarian value.

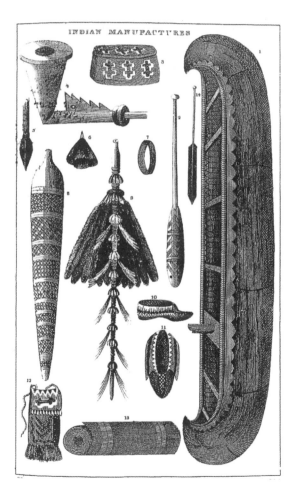

Typical handiwork of New England's Indians.

Tribes such as Maine's Passamaquoddy and Penobscot excel at weaving baskets from black ash splints and sweet grass. The most interesting of these are decorated with interweavings of porcupine quills that have been dyed in myriad colors, and softened to make them workable. The Abnaki of northern Vermont and New Hampshire are also adept at basketry and quillwork, and like many tribes have taken to working colored glass beads, acquired from white traders, into designs that grace bags, boxes, clothing, and moccasins.

You might not experience very much snowfall where you live, but that shouldn't stop you from buying a pair of snowshoes, or, as the French call them, *raquettes* (they do look like the "rackets" used in playing tennis, an aristocratic game that has yet to take root in practical-minded New England). They're made of a bent ashwood frame, over which strips of hide are woven to provide a wearer support in deep snow. A pair of this most peculiar form of footwear would be an interesting addition to any British or European cabinet of curiosities.

For the ultimate in Indian craftsmanship, though, we recommend purchasing a bark canoe. Framed with white cedar and sheathed in the bark of the white birch tree, these incredibly light and maneuverable vessels are a specialty of the Penobscot, Abnaki, and many other tribes in a region so thoroughly laced with waterways. True, transporting a canoe perhaps 14 or 16 feet in length, and carrying it aboard ship to your destination, will be no small inconvenience. But when you think of the figure you'll cut paddling the Thames or the Seine – or perhaps the Grand Canal in Venice – it will seem well worth the trouble.

IX

FESTIVITIES AND AMUSEMENTS

I n its early days, New England was anything but a festive place. The settlers, remember, were Puritans who believed that idle hands were the devil's workshop. Besides, even if their severe religion hadn't forbidden games and celebrations, they had little time left for play after spending long days carving farms and villages out of a wilderness. But the past century and a half has brought a more relaxed attitude toward innocent enjoyment, and increasing prosperity has given New Englanders more time for amusement.

During the last century, almost the only time for leisure was the interval between morning and afternoon services on the Sabbath. After all, work was forbidden on Sunday, so townspeople had to come up with some way of filling the hours between one long sermon and the other. This they did by discreet socializing, conversation, and perhaps sharing meals. But any form of sport or entertainment was out of the question.

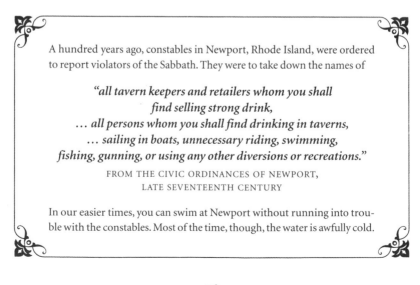

A hundred years ago, constables in Newport, Rhode Island, were ordered to report violators of the Sabbath. They were to take down the names of

"all tavern keepers and retailers whom you shall
find selling strong drink,
… all persons whom you shall find drinking in taverns,
… sailing in boats, unnecessary riding, swimming,
fishing, gunning, or using any other diversions or recreations."

FROM THE CIVIC ORDINANCES OF NEWPORT,
LATE SEVENTEENTH CENTURY

In our easier times, you can swim at Newport without running into trouble with the constables. Most of the time, though, the water is awfully cold.

SOME FAVORITE HOLIDAYS

Things have changed quite a bit over the past hundred years. Listening to the Sunday sermons – and talking about them afterwards – is no longer New Englanders' main source of amusement. The Sabbath is still kept pretty quietly in these colonies, but there are now plenty of secular occasions on which spirits run high – and flow freely.

Election days are a festive time in New England. In Massachusetts and New Hampshire, representatives, or "deputies," to the colonies' general assemblies are elected once a year on a day in early spring. Connecticut and Rhode Island hold their elections twice a year, in spring and fall – possibly because townspeople enjoy the occasion so much that it seems a shame to wait twelve whole months for the next get-together. On election days, farmers from outlying areas take the day off and head into town. After voting, they spend hours in and around the meetinghouse talking politics, crops, and the weather, and catching up on the news with their fellow citizens. Later in the day, the taverns are full.

Even if you're just passing through town on an election day, it's worth listening in on these discussions to pick up the local flavor – and if you're the sort who mingles easily, you'll eventually be asked to share a tankard of beer and a slice or two of election cake. This is a delicacy that first appeared, as far as

Election day, a time to gossip and talk politics with fellow citizens.

anyone can recall, in and around Hartford, Connecticut, and it's become almost as important a tradition as voting itself throughout New England.

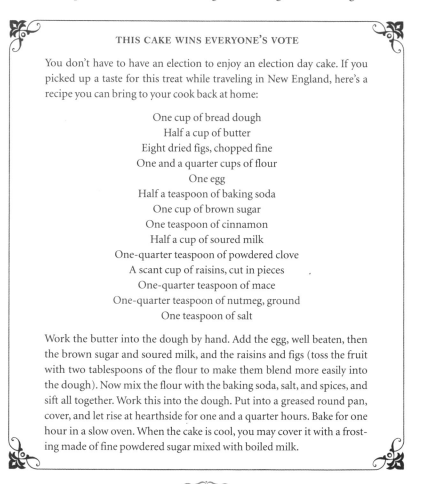

THIS CAKE WINS EVERYONE'S VOTE

You don't have to have an election to enjoy an election day cake. If you picked up a taste for this treat while traveling in New England, here's a recipe you can bring to your cook back at home:

One cup of bread dough
Half a cup of butter
Eight dried figs, chopped fine
One and a quarter cups of flour
One egg
Half a teaspoon of baking soda
One cup of brown sugar
One teaspoon of cinnamon
Half a cup of soured milk
One-quarter teaspoon of powdered clove
A scant cup of raisins, cut in pieces
One-quarter teaspoon of mace
One-quarter teaspoon of nutmeg, ground
One teaspoon of salt

Work the butter into the dough by hand. Add the egg, well beaten, then the brown sugar and soured milk, and the raisins and figs (toss the fruit with two tablespoons of the flour to make them blend more easily into the dough). Now mix the flour with the baking soda, salt, and spices, and sift all together. Work this into the dough. Put into a greased round pan, cover, and let rise at hearthside for one and a quarter hours. Bake for one hour in a slow oven. When the cake is cool, you may cover it with a frosting made of fine powdered sugar mixed with boiled milk.

"This being the day for the choice of deputies, we are told that there is a very great resort of people of all kinds and that it is a day of great frolicking ... I must observe that a man on horseback passed by with a very large bag full of cakes which are to be sold to the people."

THOMAS VERNON, A BRITISH OFFICIAL COMMENTING ON
ELECTION DAY IN A SMALL RHODE ISLAND TOWN

Boston Common, site of town celebrations and militia drills.

In towns all across New England, the half-dozen or so days set aside for
militia drills are another occasion for merriment. This might not have been
true when the militias had the hard task of keeping the Indians or the French
at bay, but in these peaceful times, training-day festivities last longer than any
actual drill practice. You'll see feats of strength, target shooting, and athletic
contests on the village green. Beer and rum flow throughout the day, and the
ladies join in for dances in the evening.

Boston holds the greatest militia event in all New England. If you're in the
city on the first Monday in June, there isn't any way you can remain unaware
of Artillery Election Day, the annual celebration of the city's Great Artillery
Company. The solemn purpose of the day is the commissioning of the company's new officers on Boston Common, and it's attended by a grand parade
including the governor and other high officials of the colony, the firing of the
State House cannon, and a sumptuous dinner at magnificent Faneuil Hall. A
casual traveler in Boston isn't likely to be invited – but for consolation, there's
always ginger beer and, yes, election cake for sale on the Common.

Other popular New England holidays include the King's Birthday, traditionally celebrated in May (though the present monarch, newly crowned King George III, was born in June) with a militia drill, cannon salute, and fireworks; and of course Guy Fawkes Day. Every Englishman knows the fifth of November as the day of the Gunpowder Plot, when the Catholic Guy Fawkes was caught trying to blow up the king and parliament in 1605. The thwarting of the plot is commemorated in the colonies as well, with parades of costumed young men and boys carrying straw effigies of Fawkes and the Pope – and begging "for a little money / To buy my Pope some drink." After dark, New England skies are lighted by great bonfires, fed, as in England, with those villains made of straw.

LIGHTING UP THE SKY

A display of fireworks is known as an "illumination." A recent development is the Italian invention of self-propelled shells that explode in color after reaching a great height.

As in Britain and most countries on the continent – and throughout the American colonies – the punishment and execution of criminals is a popular public diversion. Hangings can always draw a crowd – especially when the unfortunate soul on the gallows has had a lurid and closely watched career. In seaport towns, you can always expect a good turnout for the hanging of a pirate. But one of the most shocking crimes in recent memory – leading to one of the best-attended executions – was the 1755 poisoning of Captain John Codman of Charlestown by his two slaves, Mark and Phillis. After the pair were convicted of putting arsenic in the captain's porridge and chocolate, they were executed on Charlestown Common. Mark was hanged, and Phillis was strangled, then burned at the stake.

The crowd went home, but one of the culprits remains. If you stroll up to the execution place today, you'll see Mark's mummified body, dangling in chains above the Common.

DECEMBER 25? A DAY LIKE ANY OTHER

New Englanders enjoy all sorts of excuses for a celebration – but these don't include Christmas. The original Puritan ban on celebrating the holiday was lifted years ago, but nearly all colonists take pride in going about their usual business on a holiday that, to them, still has a Popish if not outright pagan flavor. The only notable exception is among the Church of England observers in and around Narragansett, Rhode Island. Like their Anglican brethren in the southern colonies, they feast and revel for two weeks at the end of each year.

Many visitors to these colonies have heard that New Englanders celebrate a great harvest feast each year, which they call Thanksgiving. It is true that the Pilgrim settlers of Plymouth and their Indian benefactors held such a feast to give thanks to God for their survival and first harvest, but it has by no means become an annual observance. Sometimes an individual town, or perhaps a colony government, will proclaim a day of Thanksgiving if the year's harvest has been especially bountiful, but the event is unlikely more than two or three times in a decade. A New England Yankee is not the sort to set a groaning table in both good years and bad, and we doubt he ever will be.

"There is a custom amongst us of making an entertainment at husking Indian corn whereto all the neighboring swains are invited and after the corn is finished they, like the Hottentots, give three cheers or huzzas, but cannot carry in the husks without a Rhum bottle."

DEDHAM, MASSACHUSETTS, RESIDENT NATHANIEL AMES, 1760S

MUSIC AND DANCING

It doesn't have to be a holiday for New Englanders to kick up their heels – as long as the day's work is done. As you travel from town to town, you'll always be in hearing distance of some sort of music, no matter how humble the circumstances. In the countryside, someone is sure to take out a fiddle after a house- or barn-raising, or a corn husking bee. Even the churches, in which music of any sort was once forbidden, now take pride in their hymn singing, and many can boast at least one member who can play upon the "Lord's fiddle," which you may know better as the bass viol.

It's always pleasant to find that you've arrived at a town at the same time as a group of traveling musicians. These itinerant performers make a regular circuit of some fifteen or twenty larger New England towns, giving concerts and playing for community dances. Even when a village is too small to be on the professionals' route, that fellow with the fiddle is nearly always available

Faneuil Hall, Boston's favored indoor meeting-place.

to bring the livelier set to their feet. Today's popular country dances include "High Betty Martin," "Rolling Hornpipe," "Old Father George," and "Leather the Strap." And when the dancers tire, the ballad singers take over, leading the assembly with the latest tunes learned from musical broadsides pasted onto tavern walls. Some celebrate our recent victories against the French; others strike a bawdier note. "Our Sally is a Sad Slut" might not be to the parson's taste, but it's a popular ditty of the moment.

In the big cities, you'll find more sophisticated entertainment. There are church organs now in Boston, Salem, and Newport, making divine service as uplifting musically as it is for the spirit. For secular music, Boston – as you might expect – is the most important locale. Several concerts are given each year at the city's popular dancing schools, and outdoor music programs are regularly presented at the British Coffee House, at King's Chapel, and at Faneuil Hall. Concerts at this splendid venue start at six in the afternoon on announced days, and the price of admission is never more than a dollar. There's also a new concert hall in Boston, built in 1754 especially for performances by two accomplished Anglican church organists, the brothers Lewis and Gilbert Deblois.

Devotees of military music are seldom without entertainment in Boston. Bostonians may chafe at the stationing of so many British regulars around town, but they're great aficionados of the regiments' band music – especially the free concerts given by the Sixty-Fourth.

THE STAGE IS NOT SET

One diversion you won't be able to enjoy in New England is the theater. Even though local attitudes towards leisure and amusement have loosened considerably since early Puritan days, laws banning playacting are still in force. Every now and then, someone tries to get around the rules, or at least hopes to escape notice, as when two itinerant English actors put on a performance of Thomas Otway's tragedy "The Orphan" in a Boston coffeehouse about ten years ago. The magistrates were caught napping – but not for long. Within a matter of days, "The Orphan" was just that, abandoned and forgotten.

Theaters and playgoing may still be outlawed in New England, but that hasn't stopped clever promoters from disguising dramatic performances – even quite famous ones – as moral lessons, in hopes the authorities might approve. This playbill describes a recent example of this subterfuge, staged at the King's Arms Tavern in Newport, Rhode Island:

On Monday, June 10th, at the Public Room of the above inn
will be delivered a series of

MORAL DIALOGUES
in Five Parts
Depicting the evil effects of jealousy and other bad passions
and Proving that happiness can only spring from the pursuit
Of Virtue.

Mr. Douglass – Will represent a noble and magnanimous Moor
called Othello, who loves a young lady named Desdemona, and
after he marries her, harbours (as in too many cases) the
dreadful passion of jealousy.

We needn't go on – our erudite readers will recognize the play, and wonder if Mr. Shakespeare would have appreciated being confused with a moralizing Puritan divine. Incidentally, as we go to press, we haven't heard how successful the proprietors of the King's Arms were in playing this sly gambit.

Card games, such as ombre and whist, are enjoyed by all classes.

INDOOR DIVERSIONS – AND A GAME ON THE GREEN

Many of the more worldly New Englanders you'll meet will enjoy spending an evening playing cards. Two popular games are ombre, a three-player game that originated in Spain and took fashionable Britain by storm before making its way to the colonies; and quadrille, for four players, a French adaptation of ombre more commonly enjoyed by the ladies. Both are complicated forty-card games, involving auctions, bids, alliances, and contracts, with rules too elaborate to dwell on here. It's interesting to note, though, that the game of quadrille has lately been merging, in the hands of some skilled players, with the more traditional whist. The resulting fifty-two-card hybrid is called "Boston whist" – although it originated in Europe, and not in the Massachusetts capital.

Travelers unsure of the newer games can always fall back on their knowledge of ordinary whist, or play the ever popular cribbage and backgammon. More than a few copies of Edmond Hoyle's *Treatise on Backgammon*, published in London about twenty years ago, have found their way to the colonies, and it's never difficult to find a board and strike up a game in the better city taverns and domestic parlors.

Backgammon is a popular tavern pastime.

Other tavern diversions include shovelboard, in which players try to slide weights along a long narrow table into a goal zone without shoving them too far and over the edge; and ninepins, an inn-yard game never as popular in New England as in the Dutchmen's haunts of our sister northern colonies. It's a rare public house that boasts a billiard-table, though they have appeared from time to time; and it's even more unusual to find a player adept at properly cajoling the game's four balls about the table. This will probably remain a rich man's sport, with tables to be found only in the finest private homes.

On village greens and pastures throughout New England, you're likely to see boys and young men playing various sorts of foot-ball, and also enjoying a newer ball game imported from England. It resembles the old game of rounders, which some in the southern part of England have taken to calling "base-ball," but which in America is usually just called "base." The object is simple: a player on one team throws a small, soft ball that an opposing player tries to hit with a flat-bladed bat. When the batsman hits the ball, he tries to score a "run" by rounding two base posts, while players on the opposing team try to get him "out" by throwing and hitting him with the caught ball.

Many New Englanders think that "base" is a base pastime indeed, and miss the days when their Puritan forbears would have forbidden such an idle occupation. Here is a game, they believe, better left to the less respectable sort of Yankees – the kind you might find in New York.

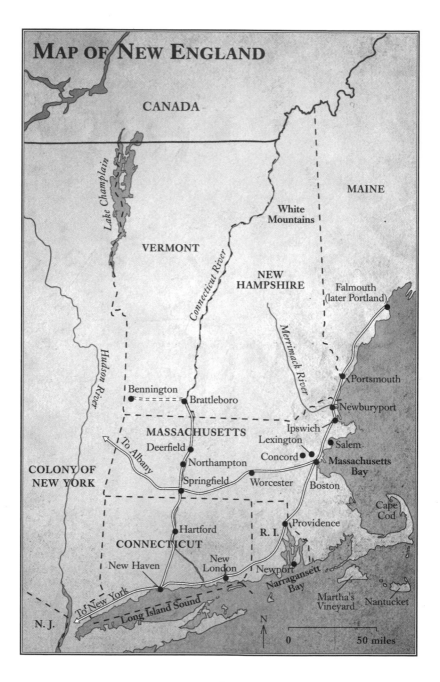

MAP OF NEW ENGLAND

CANADA

MAINE

Lake Champlain

White Mountains

VERMONT

NEW HAMPSHIRE

Connecticut River

Falmouth (later Portland)

Merrimack River

Hudson River

Portsmouth

Bennington

Brattleboro

Newburyport

MASSACHUSETTS

Ipswich

Lexington

Salem

To Albany

Deerfield

Concord

COLONY OF NEW YORK

Northampton

Massachusetts Bay

Springfield

Worcester

Boston

Cape Cod

Hartford

Providence

R. I.

CONNECTICUT

New Haven

New London

Newport

Narragansett Bay

To New York

Long Island Sound

Martha's Vineyard

Nantucket

N.J.

N

0   50 miles

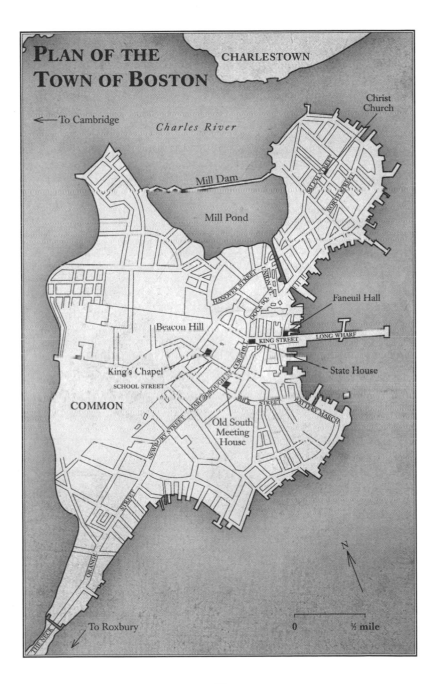

PLAN OF THE TOWN OF BOSTON

CHARLESTOWN

←—To Cambridge

Charles River

Mill Dam

Mill Pond

Christ Church

SALEM STREET

NORTH STREET

HANOVER STREET

UNION STREET

DOCK SQ.

Faneuil Hall

Beacon Hill

KING STREET

LONG WHARF

King's Chapel

CORNHILL

State House

SCHOOL STREET

MARLBOROUGH STREET

COMMON

NEWBURY STREET

DIX STREET

BATTERY MARCH

Old South Meeting House

STREET

ORANGE

N

THE NECK

To Roxbury

0   ½ mile

ACKNOWLEDGMENTS

This book could not have been written without the efforts of the countless individuals who have worked to document New England's past, and to preserve its unique character. Thanks to their dedication, I have always found it easy to slip the bounds of our own time during the many years I have lived in New England.

The guardianship of New England's colonial past has been the charge of many fine organizations, among them Historic New England (formerly the Society for the Preservation of New England Antiquities), and Salem, Massachusetts's Peabody-Essex Museum. But equal thanks must go to dozens of local historical societies, devoted to the care and interpretation of homes, taverns, and public buildings in even the most obscure corners of the region. They are the true curators of New England.

I would like to thank the staff of Bailey-Howe Library at my graduate alma mater, the University of Vermont, for saving stack space for a treasury of volumes that meticulously document the cities and towns, highways and byways, quirks and customs of colonial New England. It was at the UVM Library that I became acquainted with chroniclers such as Stewart Holbrook, Allan Forbes, and Alice Morse Earle, all of them researchers upon whose shoulders a modern writer is proud and humbled to stand.

Special gratitude goes to my old friend John J. Collins, Jr., who provided valuable information on eighteenth-century New England craftsmen. Many years ago, the massive hearth in John's old Newburyport home seemed a portal into another dimension – the dimension I have tried to portray in this book.

Finally, I thank my wife, Kay, a Massachusetts native who has been a wonderful companion along thousands of miles of rambles down the back roads of this ancient and beautiful domain. This book is dedicated to her.

SOURCES OF ILLUSTRATIONS

Key: a = above; b= below; l = left; r = right

akg/North Wind Picture Archives 33; From Bohn, Henry G. ed., *The Handbook of Games*, London 1860 137; Boston Public Library, Massachusetts 27; Child's Gallery, Boston 68; Massachusetts Historical Society, Boston 40b; Museum of Fine Arts, Boston: 30.76d 15, 30.76c 40a, Gift of Joseph W. Revere, William B. Revere, and Edward H.R. Revere, 1930, 30.781 71, The M. and M. Karolik Collection, 1939, 39.241 103, Bequest of Maxim Karolik, 1964, 64.456 114, Gift of Mrs. Nathaniel Thayer, 1931, 31.139 123; Harvard University Portrait Collection, Cambridge, Massachusetts, Bequest of Ward Nicholas Boylston, 1828 65; Chipstone Foundation Collection 67; Courtesy Concord Museum, Massachusetts 131; New Hampshire Historical Society, Concord, Massachusetts 24; Dover Publications 106; From Drake, Samuel Adams, *Old Landmarks of Boston*, Boston, 1883 49; Photo Federal Writers' Project of Massachusetts 50; Connecticut Historical Society, Hartford 69, 70, 111; From *Historic Boston*, Winchester, Massachusetts (Rawding Distributing Co.), 1964 122; Kean Collection/Getty Images 87; Victoria and Albert Museum, London 8, 136; Photo © Alice Mainville 60; From *Bibliotheca Chalcographica*, 1669 19; From *The Massachusetts Magazine; or, Monthly Museum of Knowledge and Rational Entertainment*, I, 3 March 1789, frontispiece 134; Mather, Cotton, *The Wonders of the Invisible World: Being an Account of the Tryals of Several Witches Lately Executed in New-England*, London, 1693 55; *The New-England Courant*, 1722 119; Yale University Art Gallery, New Haven, Connecticut: Mabel Brady Garvan Fund 1955.5.6 41, Gift of Jesse Lathrop Moss, B.A. 1869 100; Metropolitan Museum of Art, New York: Rogers Fund 44.29 124, Gift of Mrs. Russell Sage, 1909 72; New York Public Library 31a;

INDEX

Title page: Detail from a Paul Revere engraving of Boston.

First published in 2010 in paperback in the United States of America by Thames & Hudson Inc., 500 Fifth Avenue, New York, New York 10110

thamesandhudsonusa.com

Library of Congress Catalog Card Number 2010923258

ISBN 978-0-500-28893-1

Printed in China by Toppan Leefung